ALASKA BUSH PILOT

BY CHARLES COOMBS
ILLUSTRATED BY RAYMON NAYLOR
MAPS BY PAUL HAZELRIGG

PURPLE HOUSE PRESS KENTUCKY

More aviation books
from Purple House Press

Sabre Jet Ace
by Charles Coombs

Jenny: The Airplane that Taught America to Fly
by David Weitzman

Published by
Purple House Press
PO Box 787
Cynthiana, Kentucky 41031

Classic Books for Kids and Young Adults
purplehousepress.com

Written in 1963 by Charles Coombs
Copyright © 2024 by Purple House Press
On the cover, Ben Eielson is shown in front of
what would later be named Mt. Eielson.
All rights reserved

ISBN 9798888180761 Paperback
ISBN 9798888180778 Hardcover

CONTENTS

First Wings
1. Air Cadet — 1
2. Ben Tries Again — 8
3. The Flying Jenny — 14
4. Barnstorming — 22
5. Flying in his Blood — 33

The Far North
6. North to Alaska — 40
7. A Business Deal — 50
8. The Flying Professor — 61
9. Bush Pilot — 70
10. Airmail — 78
11. On Silver Wings — 87

Arctic Adventure
12. Clipped Wings — 94
13. Trouble at the Start — 101
14. More Hard Luck — 109
15. A Close Call — 119
16. Too Late — 124
17. A Second Try — 129
18. Stormbound — 137
19. A Hike for Life — 142

Top of the World
20. The Winning Spirit — 149
21. On to Spitsbergen! — 153
22. The Long Flight — 160
23. Green Harbor — 168
24. The Heroes Return — 177
25. Bottom of the World — 184

Back to Alaska
26. The *Nanuk* — 190
27. Folded wings — 198

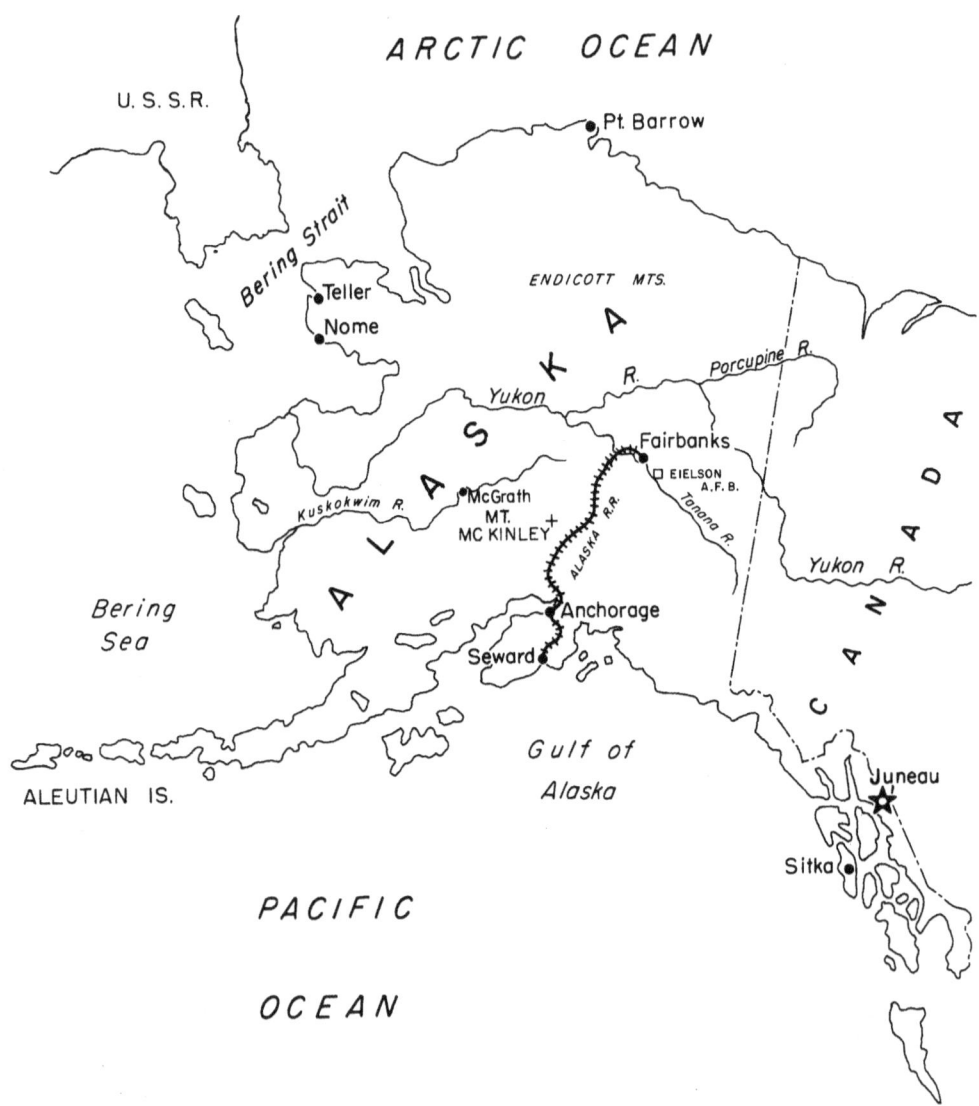

AIR CADET
CHAPTER 1

THE ENGINE hummed as the airplane flew through the clear California sky. Air Cadet Carl Ben Eielson held the control stick between his long legs. He reached down, picked up a folded map, and spread it open on his lap. The wind from the spinning propeller blew into the open cockpit and nearly tore the map from his hands.

Young Ben looked out over the edge of the cockpit. His blue eyes peered through his goggles, searching the ground far below. It spread out like a giant colored map. There were green hills, silver streams, wide grassy valleys, and tiny farmhouses. It was a pretty sight to look upon from his high flying airplane.

But something was wrong!

Nothing that he saw on the ground matched the markings on his map. Suddenly Ben knew what had gone wrong. He bit his lower lip until he nearly cried out with pain.

"I've done it again," he yelled into the wind. "I'm lost!"

Ben glanced at the instrument panel in front of him. The compass showed he was flying south.

"So what?" he thought. "If I don't know where I am, what difference does it make whether I am going south or north or east or west?"

West? That was it. If he flew west, he should come to the wide Sacramento River.

Ben wiped a drop of engine oil from his broad, slightly flat nose. He smiled, but it was a grim smile which hid his white even teeth.

"Even a fellow who has trouble finding his way out of a telephone booth should be able to find something as big and long as the Sacramento River," he said to himself. "If I can find the river, I can follow it to the city of Sacramento. From there I can fly along the highway to Mather Field. If I am really lucky, my instructor will never know that I got lost again on this cross-country training flight. If he does find out, he may wash me out as a cadet."

Luck did not seem to be on Ben's side. He flew west all right, and he came to the Sacramento River. He had just started to follow it north toward the city when the engine of his airplane began to sputter.

Ben glanced quickly at his gas gauge. His heart beat faster. The gauge read EMPTY.

"Oh, no!" Ben yelled. "What else can go wrong?"

He soon found out. The engine sputtered for the last time and died. The propeller stopped spinning. Ben looked down again. Below him thick woods lined the banks of the river.

"I can't land in those trees," he told himself. "I will crack up for sure. Maybe I will even get killed."

He looked down at the ground. It seemed very close.

"I can't be more than five hundred feet up!" Ben exclaimed. "If I don't find a clear place to land in a hurry, I'm done for!"

Then he saw a short strip of light-colored earth sticking up in the middle of the river,

"A sandbar," Ben thought. "It's not very long and not very big, but maybe it is big enough to land this plane on. I'll have to try. At least there are no trees on the sandbar to crash into."

He fastened his safety belt and glided down over the river. The wind whistled through the wire braces of the Curtiss JN-4 "Jenny" training plane.

"Easy now," Ben told himself. "Easy, boy! Do it right or you'll land in the water. Then you will be washed out and washed up." He braced his body against the back rest.

The Jenny's wheels skimmed the water and touched down on the sandbar. The plane hit hard, bouncing back into the air. It hit again, then started to roll.

Luckily the sand was solid enough so that the wheels did not sink in. Slowly the plane came to a stop at the far end of the sandbar,

Ben climbed out of the cockpit. "Well, at least I didn't crack up. But it's almost as bad. Here I am stuck in the middle of a river. How can I ever get the airplane off this sandbar?"

He looked around. A road ran along the near bank of the river. Several automobiles had stopped. People now stood at the edge of the water, staring at the strange sight of an air plane parked on a sandbar out in the middle of the river.

One man shouted, "Need any help out there?"

Ben smiled to himself. "I need help, all right," he thought. "Lots of help. What a mess I got myself into this time!"

There was only one thing to do. He took off his goggles, leather helmet, and heavy flying coat. He dived into the water and swam to shore.

As he climbed out of the water, the people crowded around him.

"You all right?"

"Here, put on my coat. You'll catch cold."

"You sure picked a funny place to land your airplane, young fellow."

"It was the best I could do," Ben said. "When my engine quit, I didn't have much time to choose."

"Say, you're a United States Army flier, aren't you?"

"Yes, sir. I'm an air cadet from Mather Field."

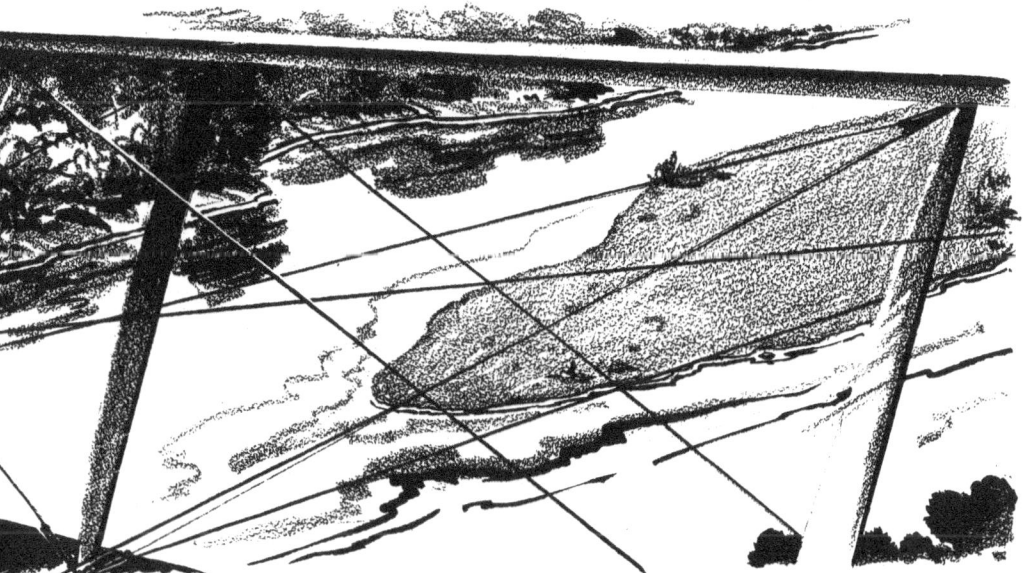

"How come you're not in France fighting the war?"

"That's what I'm training for," Ben said. "But after this—well, I've had trouble before getting lost. They may wash me out of my class."

One man looked at Ben standing there dripping wet. He laughed. "You look pretty well washed right now, young fellow."

It was not funny to Ben. He was worried. He looked back at the army Jenny parked out in the middle of the river. Even if he could get more gasoline, he would never be able to take off from that small sandbar. Much as he hated the idea, he knew what he had to do.

"Is there a telephone around here?" he asked.

"There's one about two miles down the road," one man said. "Hop in my automobile and I'll drive you."

On the telephone Ben asked for Mather Field, the army training base near Sacramento.

"Hello," a voice said over the telephone.

"Hello," Ben answered. "This is Cadet Eielson. I have had a bit of trouble, and—"

"Eielson!" the voice yelled. "Eielson, where in the world are you? You were due back here at the field an hour ago!"

Ben took a deep breath and told his flying instructor what had happened. When he had finished, there was a long silence at the other end of the line. Then the telephone nearly jerked out of Ben's fingers as his instructor shouted over the wire, "Stay where you are. Don't touch that airplane! Hear me? Don't touch it! Eielson, you can get into more trouble with an airplane than—than—oh, forget it! We'll be there as soon as we can make it."

There was a sharp click in Ben's ear as the instructor hung up the telephone.

BEN TRIES AGAIN
CHAPTER 2

It took most of the day to load the Jenny onto a boat and get it to shore where it could be filled with gas and flown back to Mather Field.

"I'll fly it," the instructor said firmly. "You might get lost again, Cadet Eielson."

Ben sat quietly in the front cockpit. The instructor in the rear cockpit flew the plane back to the training base.

The next days were grim ones for Ben. Many of his fellow cadets had finished their cross-country flights. Some of them were sent to another air base for final flight training. Then they were ready to go to France to fly and fight against the Germans in World War I. One day as Ben came in from a training flight, his instructor called him aside. Although he had passed his test, he had nearly been lost again.

"Cadet Eielson," his instructor said, "why do you keep trying to be a flier?"

"I have always wanted to be a flier," Ben said, "ever since I saw an airplane land in a big hayfield near my home in Hatton, North Dakota."

"But you are not a natural-born flier, Eielson. You know that, don't you?"

Ben could not answer a question like that. "I—I try, sir," he said, sticking out his square jaw.

His instructor smiled. "Yes, you do," he agreed, "you try very hard. That is why I haven't washed you out of training school before this. You do have a good head on your shoulders. The landing you made on that river sandbar was a smart idea. It saved Uncle Sam an airplane to say nothing of your own neck. But, Eielson, maybe you should try something else besides flying."

"Sir," Ben said, "flying is all I want to do, and the United States needs fliers in France to help win the war."

"All right, Eielson," his flying instructor said, "I'll go along with you as far as I can, but don't get lost again or in any more bad fixes. If you do, I will have to wash you out."

"Yes, sir," Ben said. "Thank you, sir."

Perhaps Ben was not a natural flier, but he made up for it by trying his best. He learned to read his maps. He learned to keep a close watch on his compass.

Weeks went by without Ben's getting lost a single time.

"You're doing fine, Cadet Eielson," his instructor said. "Keep it up. Soon you may be sent on for training in faster airplanes. Then you will be ready to go to France to help win the war."

"That is what I want, sir," Ben said happily.

"You'll have to hurry," his instructor added. "This morning's newspaper said that the Allies have the upper hand now. The war may not last much longer. Let's hope and pray that it doesn't. Hundreds of people are being killed or wounded every day."

Ben glanced at the 1918 calendar hanging on the wall. It was already November.

"If I could hurry over there," Ben said, "maybe I could help finish up the war by Christmas."

"I like your spirit, Eielson," his instructor said. "Just keep at your flight training. We'll send you over as soon as we feel you're ready to go, not before."

Ben wondered when that time would be. He was eager to go. After all, his last few flights had been good ones. Nothing had gone wrong.

On the day of his final cross-country test he ran into a storm. Clouds were all around him. Lightning flashed, its jagged fingers stabbing the sky. Thunder crashed in his ears. Ben could not see where he was going.

"I'll have to trust to my instruments," he told himself. "I must watch my compass and keep track of the time I travel in each direction. If I fail this test, I may never get to France to help the Allies win the war."

He flew carefully. The storm bounced the airplane up and down until Ben thought it would shake apart. Strong winds nearly tore the wings from the Jenny, but Ben kept his eyes on his instruments.

"I should be almost over the field," he thought finally. "Let's hope so." He crossed his fingers for good luck.

Slowly he worked his way down through the clouds. Finally he broke into the clear. He looked around, wondering where he was. Then he saw the airfield off to his right.

"Hot dog!" he yelled. "I made it! Almost on the nose. I must have passed my test this time. France, here I come!"

"Not yet, Eielson," his instructor said a few days later. "You need more training in faster airplanes like the ones being used in France."

"That's fine with me, sir," Ben said. "As long as I can get it over with in a hurry. This war might not last."

His instructor looked at him sharply. "You want the war to last, Eielson?"

"Oh, no, sir," Ben said quickly. "I didn't mean it that way. But if it does last, I want to do my part."

His instructor smiled. "You may not be the world's best pilot, Eielson," he said, "but you might be its most eager one. Anyway keep at it. We'll send you to France as soon as we know you are ready."

Ben flew almost every day. He kept waiting for his orders to send him to France. Finally they came.

"Hurrah!" Ben shouted. "At last!"

But before he could get packed, the war ended. On November 11, 1918, the Germans and the Allies laid down their guns and stopped fighting. No more airplanes flew out to shoot each other down.

All the world cheered the new peace.

Ben cheered wildly with the others. The war was over. The killing had stopped. It would be wonderful to go back home. It would be great to see his father and his brothers and sisters. Ben thought of his home as a happy one, but one important thing would be missing. There were no airplanes in Hatton, North Dakota.

Ben had his heart set upon flying. More than anything else in the world he wanted to be a flier.

THE FLYING JENNY
CHAPTER 3

EVEN THOUGH the war was over, Ben finished his flight training. He wanted to stay in the Army Air Service, but with the war over there was little need for fliers. Everyone was going home, and Ben went back to Hatton.

Ole Eielson, Ben's father, greeted him with a big bear hug. "It's good to have you back, Son," he said happily. "I hope you have had your fill of flying. Flying is meant for birds, Ben. Men would be born with wings if they were meant to fly."

Ben smiled. "We weren't born with wheels, Dad," he said, "but we drive automobiles."

Ole Eielson had never wanted his son to become a flier. When Ben left college to join the Army Air Service, his father had barely been able to hide his hurt. Being a good father though, he had allowed his son to make up his own mind. Now Ben did not want to hurt him again by saying that he wanted to keep on flying. Ole Eielson said the blessing that night at the dinner table, "…and thank you, Lord, for stopping the war and bringing our Ben safely back home to us."

After dinner the family went into the large living room. It was a gay night. Ben's four sisters and two brothers had many questions to ask. It was not long until the talk turned to Ben's plans for the future.

"First I will get a job," Ben said.

"What about school, Son?" his father asked. "You were doing fine in law school before the war took you away."

"I'm not sure I would make a good lawyer, Dad," Ben said.

"Ben, you're twenty-two years old," his older sister, Elma, said. "You should be making up your mind what you really want to do."

Ben knew that Elma was right. She usually was. Their mother had died when Ben was fourteen. Elma had been "mother" to the family ever since. She was wise and wonderful.

Still Ben could not make up his mind to go back to school. He took a job in his father's store, but he could not get airplanes out of his mind. He talked about flying whenever he got the chance.

There were many young fellows around Hatton

who were eager to listen. Like Ben, several of them were Norwegian, with the Vikings' love of adventure in their blood. They listened carefully as Ben told them how wonderful it was to fly above the clouds. Their mouths hung open when he told them about doing loops, tailspins, barrel rolls, and other flying stunts.

"But you need an airplane to fly, Ben," his friend Garvin Olson said. "Airplanes cost a lot of money. Nobody has that much money."

Neither did Ben have the money, but he had an idea. "Each of us has some money, Garv," he said. "If we put it all together, we might have enough to make the first payment on an airplane. The army is selling its old training planes. We could buy a Jenny."

"But you are the only one who knows how to fly one."

"I could teach you fellows to fly."

"Count me out," one of the others said. "I want to keep my feet on the ground."

"That's all right, too," Ben said. "An airplane can still be a good buy for us. We can earn money with it."

"How?"

"Barnstorming around the country."

"Barnstorming? What's that?"

"We'd go to county fairs, showing the airplane and putting on shows. We can take people on short rides.

Lots of people have never even seen an airplane. They will pay to see someone doing stunts. They'll pay to take rides. Quite a few ex-army pilots are buying planes and barnstorming around the country."

"Hey, it doesn't sound like a bad idea," Garvin said. "How much money would we need to get started?"

"It wouldn't take much to make the first payment on a Jenny," Ben said. "We can pay for the rest of it by putting on our shows and taking people for rides."

"Let's try it," someone else said.

Thus the Hatton Aero Club was formed in the winter of 1920. Ben's blue eyes sparkled eagerly on the day he left Hatton to buy the Jenny.

A few days later he returned with the plane. In the meantime the other eight members of the flying club made things ready. They even ran ads in the newspaper:

TIME FLIES! WHEN WILL YOU?
TAKE A DIP IN THE CLOUDS!
AVIATION IS COMING INTO ITS OWN!

Ben landed the Jenny in a cow pasture outside of town. The other members of the Hatton Aero Club were there to meet him.

"Is everything ready?" Ben asked, climbing out of the cockpit.

For a minute no one answered. This was the first time they had been close to an airplane. They felt its thin cloth cover. They looked at the many wire braces that held the wings and tail together. They climbed up and peeked into the open cockpit and asked about the control stick, rudder pedals, throttle, and the few instruments. They wondered whether they had used their money wisely.

"Will it really fly, Ben?" one of them asked.

Ben smiled. "Well, I didn't swim here," he said. "You saw me come flying in, didn't you?"

"Everyone is waiting at the ball park," Garvin said. "We told them you were going to put on a stunting show today."

"Then what am I waiting for?" Ben asked. He climbed into the cockpit.

One of the club members spun the propeller. The engine sputtered, then started. Ben waved, pushed the throttle forward, and bounced across the rough pasture for a take-off. Ben flew toward town. The Jenny roared as he dived low over the ball park. He looked down upon a sea of faces. Suddenly he did a loop right over the ball park.

"Ben's going to crash!" a man on the ground shouted as the Jenny went up, over the top, then started down.

"The plane will fall apart!"

A woman screamed.

Ben did not hear any of this. He sat in the cockpit, smiling, as the plane finished its loop.

For the next few minutes Ben put on a show that the people of Hatton were never to forget. He did loops, dives, barrel rolls, tailspins, and sideslips. He made the Jenny do everything it could without tearing off its wings.

The wind whistled through the wires as the plane went into another screaming dive. The engine roared. It was like music to Ben's ears.

He loved to fly, and he was flying!

He looked at the gas gauge. "Wow," he said, "the tanks are nearly empty. I'd better land."

There was a clear field near the ball park. Ben made one last dive over the crowd. Then he landed.

The people cheered him,

"Hurrah for Ben!"

"Ben has brought aviation to North Dakota!"

"Ben is our flying pioneer!"

Everyone seemed happy. Everyone seemed thrilled, all but one, that is.

Ole Eielson made his way through the crowd. He stood at the side of the Jenny as Ben climbed out of the cockpit.

"Hello, Dad," Ben said. "How did you like the show?"

Ole Eielson tried to smile. Then Ben saw the tears in his father's eyes.

"What's the matter. Dad?" he asked.

His father put his arm around Ben's shoulders. "You be careful, Son," he said. "You be very careful." Ole Eielson looked at the airplane as though it were his worst enemy. "That thing could kill you, Ben. It could kill you!"

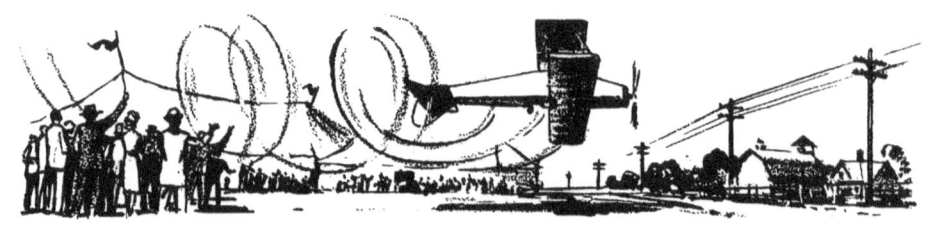

BARNSTORMING
CHAPTER 4

A FEW WEEKS later Ben flew the Jenny over a county fairground in the Middle West. He looked down at the mass of faces.

"From up here they always seem to look the same," he told himself.

Something was bothering him. He was not sure what it was. A large number of persons were watching the show today. There had been big crowds at most of the county fairs where he had put on his flying shows that summer of 1920.

Yet something was wrong.

Ben did a loop while the people below looked on. He did a barrel roll close to the ground. A woman screamed when the Jenny's wing tips nearly touched the ground.

Men shouted in alarm when Ben flew under some

telephone wires at one edge of the fairgrounds. He barely missed them.

"That wasn't a very smart thing to do," Ben thought. "What made me do a foolish thing like that? I might have hit those wires. That would have wrecked the plane. I might even have been killed."

When he had gone through all his flying stunts, Ben landed the plane. He climbed out of the cockpit. He was taking off his helmet and goggles when Garvin Olson rushed up. Garvin's face was grim.

"Ben," Garvin cried out, "flying under those telephone wires was a foolish thing to do. What got into you anyway?"

Ben was trying to think of an answer when the crowd gathered around him.

"That was a real flying circus you put on today, Eielson," a man called. "It was well worth what I paid to see it."

"Eielson, you're a real daredevil," another shouted.

Circus! Daredevil! That was it! Suddenly Ben knew what was bothering him.

That night he paced up and down in his hotel room. Garvin Olson watched him.

Ben was usually restless on the night before a flight. He often walked the floor, and when he went to bed, he got little sleep. He talked and sometimes even walked in his sleep. This was what happened the night before a flight. Now Ben was restless on the night after a flight.

"What's bothering you, Ben?" Garvin asked finally.

Ben looked at his friend. "Flying is more than a circus, Garv," he said. "I don't like being called a daredevil."

"If flying under those telephone wires today wasn't being a daredevil, what is?"

"I made a mistake, Garv. I shouldn't have done it. The point is that aviation is more than what we are doing."

"We are not doing so badly," Garvin said. "For months now we've been barnstorming all over the Middle West. We have had good days and bad days, but we have made money. The Jenny is nearly paid for. Everyone in the club is happy. What is so bad about barnstorming?"

"The country is full of barnstormers, Garv. There are good daredevils and bad daredevils. Some do all right. Some crack up. Some get killed. People are beginning to think that aviation is no more than putting on a stunt show."

"You always put on a good show, Ben."

"I would like to prove that airplanes can be used for a lot more things than putting on shows, Garv."

"Things like what?"

"Well, like sending letters across our country by airplane."

"We have some airmail," Garvin reminded him. "It started a year or so ago."

"They're short hops, Garv. Why not have cross-country airmail? Why not fly the mail all the way from New York to California?"

"Ben, you're dreaming! No plane could begin to fly that far."

"We can make planes that will fly that far," Ben said. "We can put more gas tanks in them."

"What else, Ben?"

"We can carry more people. We can carry them farther and faster. Maybe we can carry twenty-five or fifty passengers at a time."

"That would take a mighty big plane, Ben!"

"Then we should make big planes. We could use some to carry people and others to carry cargo. We could fly medicine, machinery, food, things like that. We could use airplanes to explore places you can't reach any other way."

"What places, Ben?"

"Oh there is still a lot of wild country right here in the United States. There is more of it in Canada, and—and Alaska."

"Alaska? 'Way up there near the Arctic Circle? Ben,

that's bush country, really wild country. It's all snow and ice. There are great plains called tundra that are either frozen in the winter or swampy in the summer. There are freezing storms that would tear the wings off an airplane. The mountains are so high and jagged a plane couldn't get over them. What good would an airplane be in Alaska, Ben?"

"Oh, I've heard that a few planes have reached Alaska already," Ben said.

"Most of them have crashed, too," Garvin reminded Ben. "I don't blame you for dreaming about all those things, but right now we're busy barnstorming. Maybe we'd better keep our minds on that for a while."

Ben knew his friend was right. It was not good to have your mind full of other things when you were barnstorming. You had to think every minute to keep out of danger.

During the next few weeks Ben and Garvin flew to different towns, from fairground to fairground. They did one flying show after another.

Garvin planned the shows and took care of the money. He helped Ben keep the airplane in good flying order. Often he helped Ben start the Jenny by spinning the propeller.

Some days Ben could not fly because the weather was bad. Some days the fields were too wet or too muddy for landing or taking off. Some days the engine would sputter and fail to start. Then the people were given back their money.

One day the engine quit while Ben was giving a show. He looked around for a place to land. On the far side of some railroad tracks he saw a small pasture with trees and bushes on it. There was one short cleared strip that he thought was big enough to land the Jenny. At least he had to try.

He glided toward it. The wind whistled through the wire braces. The plane bounced up and down in the air currents.

Suddenly before him were two rows of telephone poles, one on each side of the railroad tracks. Wires stretched between the poles. He had to get over them to reach the clearing.

With its dead engine the Jenny already had glided down low, maybe too low to get over the wires. It was too late for Ben to change his mind. There was no other place to land. He glided toward the first row of wires and barely missed them. The railroad tracks flashed beneath his wheels.

The second row of wires loomed up. Ben braced himself. The Jenny's tail skid caught for a moment on one of the wires. Then it broke free.

Ben landed on the pasture. The Jenny bounced once, rattling Ben's teeth. The wheels sank in soft mud. The plane slid forward on its nose, almost tipping over. Then it fell back on its tail skid.

Ben was shaken up, but he was not hurt.

"Boy," he said to himself, "that was a close call."

The next day Ben and Garvin Olson went back to the pasture to get their plane. By the time they had fixed the engine, a crowd of people had gathered to see what they were doing.

"This pasture is too soft for taking off, Ben," Garvin said. "The wheels will sink in."

"We can take some gas out of the tanks," Ben said.

"That will make the Jenny lighter. Over there is some fairly dry ground. Maybe I can take off from that."

Some of the men in the crowd helped push the Jenny to the far end of the pasture. Then they turned it around to face the railroad tracks.

"You'll have to watch the telephone wires, Ben," Garvin warned.

"I know," Ben agreed. "I can't forget how I nearly crashed into them when I landed yesterday."

He climbed into the cockpit, pulling on his helmet and goggles. Garvin went to the front of the plane and took hold of the propeller.

"Switch on?" he called.

"Switch on," Ben answered, flipping the switch.

Garvin spun the propeller. The engine started with a roar.

Ben called to the men. "Can you push on the wings? Help me get rolling over this soft ground."

"Sure, we'll help!"

The men pushed. The engine roared. The Jenny started rolling slowly across the grass of the pasture. Soon it was going faster than the men could run. One by one they let go and stood watching as the Jenny picked up speed, but the soft mud of the pasture kept the Jenny from getting up the speed it needed.

Ben looked ahead through the spinning propeller.

Straight in front of him were the railroad tracks and the two rows of telephone poles.

"Faster!" Ben shouted into the wind. "Faster!"

The wires and poles came closer and closer.

"Am I going to make it?" Ben yelled. "Am I going to get over them?"

It was too late now to stop the plane. Suddenly Ben pulled back on the control stick. The Jenny bounced once and lifted heavily.

Ben was already near the first row of wires, but the plane was only a few feet off the ground. Now Ben knew he could not get over them. He had only one choice—to go under the wires.

There was barely space for the Jenny to pass between the ground and the hanging wires and between the telephone poles. Ben held his breath as he flew the Jenny through the small space. The wings nearly touched one pole.

Then there were the railroad tracks laid on high ground. Ben pulled back hard on the control stick. The Jenny's wheels just missed the tracks. The engine roared, but the plane began to fall back toward the ground again.

"Up!" Ben shouted. "Up!"

Beyond the tracks was the second row of telephone poles. One of them was straight ahead of the plane.

Ben pushed hard on the rudder pedal. The Jenny started to turn, but it was too late.

One wing hit the pole. The plane spun around and crashed into the ground. Ben hung on for his life as the Jenny bounced into some bushes. Wires snapped. Broken wood flew all around him. Cloth tore. One wing snapped off. The Jenny finally skidded to a stop. Badly shaken up, Ben sat in the cockpit. He heard loud shouts. A crowd was running toward him with Garvin Olson in the lead. Ben started to climb out of the cockpit.

"Ben, are you all right?" Garvin cried.

"I—I think so," Ben said slowly. "But the Jenny isn't. I made a mess of it, Garv."

"You couldn't help it, Ben. You did your best. Maybe we can fix the plane again."

Ben looked at the broken wings, the smashed landing gear, and the Jenny's body all twisted out of shape.

"She'll never fly again, Garv," he said. "It looks as if this is the end of the Hatton Aero Club."

"Maybe you're right, Ben," his friend agreed. "It has been a good summer, but all things have to end sometime."

"That's right," Ben said. "It's the end of something else, too."

"What's that, Ben?"

"No more barnstorming for me," Ben said. "When I fly again, it will be for a better reason than merely stunting."

FLYING IN HIS BLOOD
CHAPTER 5

OLE EIELSON was happy to have Ben back home. He was thankful that Ben had not been hurt when the Jenny cracked up. He was glad his son's feet were again on the ground.

"I worried about you every minute you were flying, Ben," he said. "One crash is enough. You were lucky not to be killed. I hope you have had your fill of flying."

Ben did not say anything about that, but he knew he had not had his fill of flying. Far from it. Aviation was still in his blood. He loved the sound of the wind whistling through the wires. He loved the feeling of joy that flying high above the earth gave him. He was proud of all he had learned to be able to fly.

He hoped to fly again, but he did not say anything to his father about it. He did not want to worry him.

"Don't you think it's time you went back to school now, Ben?" his father asked. "The country needs good lawyers more than it needs daredevil fliers. You should finish college, Son. After all, you are twenty-three years old. If you don't do it now, you may never do it."

"You could be right. Dad," Ben agreed. "I'll go back to school."

The last year of college was not easy for Ben. He had been away from school for four years. Now he was quite a bit older than most of the other students.

He had been a star basketball player before the war. He tried playing basketball again, but it did not thrill him as it had when he was younger.

His mind kept going back to flying. He talked about flying to any student who was interested. Most students were. Every day new things were being done by airplanes.

Ben studied hard. He owed it to himself as well as to his father. He made good grades. He was proud when college ended in June, 1921. Yet he knew it would take more years of special schooling before he could become a lawyer.

He worked in Hatton during the summer months. Then he went east to Washington, D.C., to study law at Georgetown University.

To help pay his own way through school, he got a

part-time job as a guard in one of the government buildings.

One day he met a fine gentleman named Dan Sutherland. Sutherland, a member of Congress from Alaska, asked Ben, "Have you ever been to Alaska?"

"No, sir," Ben said. "I guess only a few people have been that far north."

"Right you are, Ben, and that is too bad. Alaska is a wonderful place. It's not all snow and ice as many people believe."

"Oh, snow and ice don't bother me," Ben said. "We have plenty of both in North Dakota."

"Alaska could use young men like you, Ben," Dan Sutherland went on. "There is a great future there. Believe me, Ben, I can see the day when the Territory of Alaska will become a state of the United States of America."

"Do you really think so, Mr. Sutherland? It's such a long way from any of the other states."

"I wouldn't say so if I didn't firmly believe it," the older man said. "Alaska is a mighty big place. It is more than one-fifth the size of all the states put together. The trouble is there are so few people in Alaska, Ben. It will take a lot more people and a lot of work before Alaska can earn its place among the United States."

"It sounds interesting, sir," Ben said. "But I can't seem to get my mind off flying."

It was as though he had said a magic word. "Flying!" Mr. Sutherland exclaimed. "Airplanes! You have hit the problem right on the nose, Ben. Travel is Alaska's biggest problem. There are few roads. In the winter people have to use dogsleds. In the summer they go by small, slow riverboats."

Dan Sutherland went on to tell Ben how hard it was to travel in Alaska. High mountains, deep icy rivers, and great plains of frozen or swampy tundra made travel very hard.

"It is bush country, Ben, about as hard a land to move around in as you can imagine. Maybe airplanes

are the answer. People could fly over the country instead of trying to get across it."

During the coming weeks Ben and Dan Sutherland had many talks about Alaska. Thinking of Alaska and thinking of flying sharpened Ben's love of adventure.

Little by little he lost his interest in studying law. At the end of one term he left Georgetown University and returned to Hatton.

If he was hurt because his son had left school, Ole Eielson tried not to show it.

"What will you do now, Son?" he asked.

"I will get a job for a while, Dad. Maybe I can teach school."

"That's a good idea, Ben," his father said. He seemed pleased. He had been afraid his son would start talking about flying again.

Ben worked around Hatton during the summer. He enjoyed being home with his brothers and sisters and his father. The family had many good times together.

But Ben was not happy with his job. He kept thinking about Alaska and the things Dan Sutherland had told him about the vast territory. It would be a great adventure to go there, even if he did not fly.

One day Ben received a letter from Mr. Sutherland. "The Fairbanks High School needs someone to teach English and science and to coach basketball," the letter read. "The job sounds made to order for you, Ben. As you know, Fairbanks is right in the middle of Alaska. If you would like the job, let me know."

Ben shouted, "How lucky can I be! Hey, Dad! Elma! Look at this!"

His father and older sister read the letter.

"Do you want to take the job, Ben?" his father asked.

"If you think it is all right. Dad."

"It sounds all right to me, Ben. I have heard that Alaska is the place for someone with pioneer blood, and you have the blood of Vikings in you. You have my blessing. If I were a younger man, I would go with you."

"I would like that. Dad," Ben said.

"Father is right, Ben," Elma agreed. "I know you have been restless. Alaska should be a good change. I hear there are plenty of chances for adventure there."

"I hope so," Ben said. "I will answer Mr. Sutherland's letter. Then I'd better start thinking of what to take."

"I'll help you pack," Elma offered.

"Hey," Ben laughed, "don't be so eager to get rid of me."

"Oh, Ben, how can you say that?"

"I was fooling," Ben said, giving Elma a big hug. Ben looked around. His father had gone outside.

"Elma," he said, "you don't think Dad really minds if I go, do you?"

"Oh, I'm sure he doesn't, Ben," his sister said. "Of course, he will miss you. We all will. But this will take care of Father's big worry."

"What big worry, Elma?"

"Father has been afraid that you might want to start flying again."

Ben did not say anything. He had thought of little else but flying during the past few months. He had not said anything about it for fear of worrying his father.

Elma went on, "But Father knows that Alaska is not a place for airplanes."

NORTH TO ALASKA
CHAPTER 6

IT WAS raining when Ben got off the train at the west coast port of Seattle, from which he would take a ship to Alaska. The water of the bay was gray and quiet beneath the low-hanging clouds.

The train ride from North Dakota had been long. Ben was tired. He was lonely. He was in a strange city far from home on a wet and gloomy day.

Alaska was still a long boat ride away.

Ben picked up his suitcase and started down the street. He saw an eating place and stopped to buy some hot soup. After eating, things did not seem nearly so gloomy as before.

Then he went to the docks where he would board his ship. The cold rain was still coming down. An old steamer lay tied to the dock, rocking gently in the swells. Smoke rose from its stack. Ben went up the gangplank.

"Hey, where are you going, young fellow?" A man in a seaman's cap stopped him.

"Isn't this the steamer that's going to Alaska?" Ben asked.

"That's right. Do you have a ticket?"

Ben dug into his pocket and showed the seaman his ticket.

"Good enough. But you are early, lad. We don't leave until tomorrow morning."

"I see," Ben said. "Well, I guess I'd better find a hotel for the night."

"You don't need to. You can sleep aboard ship if you want."

So Ben stayed aboard the ship, but he did not get much sleep. During the night the water of the bay turned rough. The small ship pitched up and down. It banged against the dock. At times Ben had to hold on to keep from being thrown out of his bunk.

By morning the water was smooth. With loud toots from its whistle, the ship pulled away from the dock and headed north.

For the next few days the steamer wound its way past many wooded islands through smooth water.

"This is called the Inside Passage," one of the seamen explained to Ben. "These islands shelter us from the rough waters of the Pacific Ocean."

"It's wonderful country," Ben said as he looked shoreward at the snow-capped mountains. "I thought Alaska was all ice and snow and bare tundra."

"Don't worry," the seaman said, smiling. "Plenty of it is ice and snow and tundra, but that is farther north. You see, we are still some distance from the main part of Alaska."

The next day the ship left the shelter of the Inside Passage. It headed on a westerly course across the Gulf of Alaska. The water turned rough. A cold wind chilled Ben to the bone. Most of the passengers hurried to their cabins, but Ben stayed on deck, feeling the cold salt spray on his face and the thrill of adventure in his heart. A sudden hard rainstorm at last drove him below deck with the others.

When Ben got up the next morning, the ship was feeling its way along a narrow harbor toward a cluster of buildings and a dock.

"We are coming into Seward," a seaman explained. "It's not much of a city after what you're used to seeing in the States, but for Alaska it's big. Up here people call a few log cabins and a trading post a city."

Ben watched as the ship steamed into port and dropped anchor.

He caught the first northbound train out of Seward to Anchorage, Alaska's biggest city. The train wound through high, rugged, snow-capped mountains. The tracks twisted past giant glaciers. These were vast fields of slow-moving ice which for many ages had built up between the mountain ranges.

"Hey, look!" Ben shouted suddenly, pointing out the window.

Most of the other passengers pressed their faces against the train windows. A large brown bear ran up the side of the wooded hill beside the tracks.

"That's a big one!" someone shouted.

The man sitting across from Ben did not even bother to leave his seat. He was an old fellow with a chin full of whiskers. He wore heavy boots, and his clothes looked as though they had been lived in for a long time. Ben had decided much earlier that the old gentleman was one of Alaska's pioneer miners or "sourdoughs," as they were called.

"Boy, that was some bear!" Ben said, settling back in his seat.

"Sonny," the old sourdough smiled through his whiskers, "that could be someone's house pet. If you

stay in Alaska long enough, you will see bears that will make that one look like a child's toy. You'll see other animals, too, lots of them, big and small."

"Fine," Ben said, "I like animals."

They rode on. Suddenly the train brakes jammed. The quick stop made some of the passengers fall to the floor. Ben grabbed the seat ahead of him. He looked at the sourdough, who still sat reading his newspaper.

"What happened?" Ben asked the man.

"Maybe there's a moose on the tracks," the sourdough said without looking up from his newspaper.

"Moose?"

"Or a caribou. Go have a look."

Excited, Ben jumped down from the car and ran forward along the tracks toward the engine.

"Hey, you!" the engineer called down from his high seat in the engine cab. "Get back on the train! If that bull moose takes off after you—"

Then Ben saw the reason why the train had stopped so quickly. A giant bull moose stood right in the middle of the tracks. It had its head down, facing the engine. Its great antlers had a spread well over six feet from tip to tip.

"Hurry up, young fellow," the engineer called down. "Climb up here. Quick! That moose is mad!"

Just then the moose saw Ben. It pawed the ground. Then, with a loud bellow, it charged.

Ben let out a bellow of his own and raced toward the engine. He caught hold of the grab rail and swung himself into the cab. The moose's antlers barely missed him as they banged into the side of the train.

The engineer blew the whistle and pushed the throttle. The train started forward. The angry moose was left standing beside the tracks.

The engineer turned to Ben. "I guess I should thank you," he said. "That moose might have held us up for a long time. Those big bulls can cause us a lot of trouble. Sometimes you can't get them off the tracks.

Other times they will charge and damage the train. Sometimes we don't have time to stop. We meet head on."

"Don't they hurt themselves?" Ben asked.

"You bet they do, and worse than that. Sometimes we have enough fresh moose meat to last for months."

Soon the train was following along the edge of the mud flats leading toward Anchorage.

"When the tide is in, those flats are underwater," the engineer explained. "Fishing is good too, but you have to watch the tides. If you get caught in an outgoing tide, it can sweep you out to sea before you can get your boat to shore. Is this your first time in Alaska?"

"Yes."

"Well, what do you think of it?"

"It looks pretty rugged so far."

"You are right. Alaska is rugged. It takes a man to live in this country, lad."

Ben smiled. "Oh, I don't figure to give up easily," he said.

"Well, you won't find it so bad in Anchorage anyway," the engineer said. "It's quite a large city."

"But I'm not staying in Anchorage," Ben explained. "I'm going to Fairbanks."

"You are? That's farther north," the engineer said,

"nearly four hundred miles from here. It's away up in the middle of the territory, nearly to the Arctic Circle. Living can be hard up there."

"Why?"

"The cold. It gets so cold a man has to be mighty careful how deep a breath he takes or he'll frost his lungs. If you wander out into a blizzard, you can freeze to death standing up like a fence post. In the summer the mosquitoes are so big you have to shoot them down like airplanes. You can earn good money hunting them, though."

"Earn money hunting mosquitoes?" Ben asked.

"Sure. The railroad company will buy all the stingers you can bring them."

"Mosquito stingers?" Ben wondered. "What for?"

"They use them for railroad spikes, son. Saves a lot of steel that way."

Ben laughed to think he had fallen for the engineer's joke. "I'll remember that," he said.

In a few minutes the engineer pointed through the cab window. "Well, there she is—Anchorage."

Ben looked. The city spread out on high ground above the railroad tracks. For the biggest city in Alaska, Anchorage did not seem so large. It was mostly wooden houses, log cabins, and a few stores and hotels on both sides of the muddy streets.

A chill September wind was blowing. Ben pulled his coat close around him. "Thanks for the ride in the cab," he said to the engineer.

"You're welcome," the engineer said. "Besides, you helped us out of a tight spot by letting that moose chase you instead of the train."

Ben laughed. "I didn't let him," he said. "I just didn't know any better."

The engineer said again, "Alaska is not an easy place to live. She doesn't often let you get away with more than one mistake. Don't you forget that, son, or you won't be alive long."

A chill passed along Ben's spine, and it was not caused by the wind. Already, from the little he had seen of Alaska, Ben felt that the engineer spoke wisely.

"I'll try to be careful," he said as he started back to get his suitcase.

"Be sure of it," the engineer called, "and good luck."

As he started up the hill toward town, Ben had the feeling that he was going to need all the good luck he could get in this strange new land.

A BUSINESS DEAL
CHAPTER 7

BEN DID not waste time. The next day he caught the first train going north to Fairbanks. The school year was about to start. He did not want to be late for his first teaching job.

He stared as the train wound past the foot of Mt. McKinley, the highest mountain in all North America. It pushed itself upward more than four miles into the sky, losing its white peak in the clouds.

Several times the train had to stop while the engineer tooted his whistle and rang his bell to chase moose or caribou off the tracks. On this trip Ben stayed inside the train and watched through the car windows. Being charged once by an angry moose had been enough for him.

As the train ran north along the Nenana River, the mountains became smaller and less rugged. The land was flat and spotted with many streams and lakes.

A BUSINESS DEAL

"It's hard country to get around in," the well dressed man sitting next to Ben explained. "Each town and village is far apart with nothing but mountains, brush, and tundra in between. We call it bush country," the man went on, "or just the bush."

"I have heard it is rough country," Ben said.

"You heard right. There are no roads. In the winter when the ground is frozen solid, the only way to cross it is by dogsled. In the summer much of it turns to swamp, which we call muskeg. There's no way at all to cross it then, but a man wouldn't want to. Clouds of giant mosquitoes darken the sky. I mean, they're big ones. Talk about stingers! Why, the railroads use them—"

"I know," Ben spoke up quickly, "they use them for railroads spikes."

They both laughed.

"What's your name?" the stranger asked.

"Carl Ben Eielson, but everyone calls me Ben."

"O.K., Ben it is. My name is Bill Thompson. But everyone calls me Wrong Font."

"Wrong Font?"

The other man smiled. "It's a printer's term. You see, I am editor of the Fairbanks *News-Miner*."

"A newspaper?"

"That's right. It's the only daily newspaper in all

central Alaska. Are you a trapper, a gold miner, or what?"

Ben told him about the teaching job waiting for him in Fairbanks.

"Oh, so you're the new professor. Fine. We need another good teacher. We have nearly fifty students in our high school now. Fairbanks is growing all the time."

They stayed the night in Nenana, a small town. Many of the houses were cabins or shacks. Some of them were little more than shelters dug out of the earth and roofed over.

"People don't get very fancy up in this country," Wrong Font said. "Just keeping alive is a full-time job for most,"

Nenana was less than sixty miles from Fairbanks, but it took most of the next day to cover the distance. Every few miles the train had to stop while men fixed or cleared the tracks so the train could go on.

"This country is bad for railroads," Wrong Font explained. "The mushy tundra makes a poor roadbed. Tracks get out of shape and sometimes even sink out of sight. When it's not the tundra, it's mountain slides or raging streams. The weather can be mighty rough, too. Yes, sir, people have no easy job getting around in this country, winter or summer."

"I know of an easy way to get around," Ben said, "winter or summer."

"You can't unless you've got wings," the editor said.

"That's just it. I'd do it with wings—fly—use airplanes."

Wrong Font looked at him and scratched the whiskers on his chin. "Maybe so," he said. "It might work if you could get an airplane up here. More than one pilot has crashed trying to get this far north,"

"Oh, I think it could be done," Ben said. He was not sure why he kept thinking of airplanes. After all, he had come to Alaska to teach school.

"Say," Wrong Font asked, "you don't happen to be one of those flying fellows yourself, do you?"

Ben told him about his Army Air Service days and his barnstorming adventures. The newspaper editor seemed very much interested.

When the train arrived at Fairbanks, Wrong Font Thompson shook hands with Ben. "Come to see me," he said. "Maybe we can talk a little more about that flying business. You might have a good idea there."

Ben got a room in a hotel, but he did not sleep much that night. He kept thinking about his talk with Wrong Font Thompson. Perhaps airplanes might be the answer to Alaska's biggest problem—getting from one place to another.

"Now quit thinking about airplanes," he told himself. "Your job is to teach school." Finally he dropped off to sleep.

The next morning he walked through town toward school. A chill arctic wind drove him deep into the folds of his coat.

Fairbanks, Alaska's second biggest city, was also a log-cabin town. There were some stores, hotels, and eating places, and there were many business buildings along the main streets. Some of the houses were as nice as those in Hatton, but many were cabins with dirt roofs and windows boarded up against the cold.

Fairbanks sat on a piece of high land between the small Chena River and the large Tanana River, There were plenty of trees along the river banks, in the city, and on the nearby hills. High snow-capped mountains loomed up in the distance. Between the mountain ranges there was the vast treeless tundra.

The months passed. During November, December, and January the weather was very cold. Even with steam heat in the red wooden schoolhouse, it was all a person could do to keep warm.

Ben taught English and science. He also coached the basketball team. Often it was too cold to play, for all the games had to be played outside.

More and more Ben found himself talking to his students about airplanes and what aviation could do for Alaska. They listened eagerly. Their young eyes opened wide at the thought of flying.

Several of them also found out that if the studying got too hard, all they had to do was say something about airplanes. Then Ben would forget all about the day's lesson and start talking about flying.

One night while having dinner at the hotel, Ben let his feelings be known. "I came here to teach school," he said, "but what I really want to do is fly! Alaska needs aviation."

One of the sourdoughs sitting at the table spoke up, "I'm not so sure about that, Ben. Can you fly an airplane in sixty-below-zero weather? If you touch a piece of metal with your bare hand when it's that cold, you will stick fast to it. Your skin will tear right off when you try to get loose."

"It doesn't have to be that cold for oil to freeze solid," another said. "I know. Some mornings I have to build a fire under my automobile to thaw it out. Then sometimes I can't steer it because ice has formed on all its joints. A fellow would be even worse off up in the sky in an airplane, wouldn't he?"

"I don't know," Ben said. "Those are things I would have to find out."

"You may get killed doing it," the sourdough said, "I'll stick to the dogsleds and the riverboats. They have done the job for years."

"If everyone thought that way," Ben said, "people would still be crossing the United States in covered wagons."

"Well, if you really want to fly, why don't you do something about it?"

Ben did. He remembered his talk on the train with Wrong Font Thompson. The next day after school he went to the office of the Fairbanks *News-Miner*.

"I wondered whether you were ever going to come

and see me. Professor," the editor said. "I hear you're doing fine at your teaching job."

"I'm trying," Ben said, "but I can't say my heart is really in it."

"What is your heart in?"

"Flying."

Wrong Font leaned back and smiled. "I've guessed as much. One of my neighbor boys told me how he can get you to talking about airplanes at the drop of a hat."

Ben laughed. "Yes, some of the students seem to have my number, all right."

"O.K., Ben, so you want to fly. I have been doing some thinking about it, too. You may be right. Aviation might be a big help up here. The more I think about it, the more I like the idea. I will help you. What's the first move?"

"To get an airplane," Ben said.

"Where? When? How much?"

"There are some old wartime Jennies for sale down in the States. We could order one right away."

"How much?"

"Maybe a thousand dollars, more or less."

"How much money do you have, Ben?"

"Money?" Ben said, looking down at the floor. "None. I—I'm even a week behind on my room rent at the hotel."

He knew suddenly that it had been foolish even to think of buying an airplane.

Wrong Font laughed. "I don't have much more," he said, "but I think I know where we might be able to get some money. Come on.

They hurried through the biting cold to the bank. The banker, Dick Wood, listened while Wrong Font drew a glowing word picture of what aviation could do for Alaska. Ben just listened and kept his fingers crossed.

When the newsman was finished, Dick Wood smiled. "You don't fool me with all your pretty words. Wrong Font," he said. Then he turned to Ben. "You haven't said anything yet, Professor. Tell me, what do you think about all this?"

"I think we could make an airplane pay for itself in a hurry, Mr. Wood," Ben said. "I have talked to some people up here. They would pay a good price to take a ride in an airplane. Others would pay just to watch a plane do stunts. I used to be a barnstormer."

"But people will pay only once or twice to see a flying circus. After that what?"

"Oh," Ben said quickly, "I would put on shows only to get people interested in aviation. Then we would do much more important things with the airplane."

"Like what?"

Ben took a deep breath. "We could carry mail and other things they need to far-off villages," he said eagerly. "We could take trappers to their traplines. We could fly miners to their mine diggings. We could haul all kinds of things—medicine, food, mine machinery."

"Now you're talking sense," the banker said. "That sounds good enough for me. O.K., I will agree to put in a third of the money."

"Great!" Wrong Font said. "I will put in a third. Ben will put in a third. Now, will you lend each of us enough money to do it?"

For a minute Ben thought Dick Wood would throw them both out of the building. Then the banker laughed. "Wrong Font," he said, "you drive a hard deal. In other words you want me to put up all the money!"

"Only for a while," the newspaper editor said. "We'll pay you back, won't we, Ben?"

"We certainly will," Ben said.

Dick Wood shook his head. "Maybe I'm crazy," he said, "but I'll do it."

Thus the first aviation company in the far north was formed. An order was placed for a Jenny to be shipped from the States.

Ben went back to teaching school. More months passed, but no airplane arrived.

The cold weather ended, and spring came. The ice

broke up on the rivers. The fields and hills turned brown as the snow melted and the land thawed. Green grass sprang up on the fields and in the marshes.

School ended.

Still no airplane arrived.

Then, on the first of July, 1923, a boy rushed into the hotel while Ben was having breakfast.

"Mr. Eielson," he shouted, "the train just came in. Men are unloading a lot of big boxes. They have your name on them."

Ben jumped up from the table. "It's the Jenny," he cried happily. "Our airplane has finally arrived!"

THE FLYING PROFESSOR
CHAPTER 8

PLENTY OF willing hands helped Ben haul the boxes out to the Fairbanks ball park, where the Jenny would be put together.

Most of those who helped carry stayed to watch. They shook their heads as, piece by piece, the plane was taken out of the boxes.

"That thing will never fly," one old sourdough said, grinning. "Why, it's nothing but wood and cloth."

"Look at that tiny engine," a dogsled driver said. "The first time Eielson tries to get over one of those mountains, he'll crash right into it. I'll stick to my dogs. They always take me where I want to go."

"The wind will blow that airplane thing around like a kite with a broken string," another said.

Ben tried not to listen. The Jenny did look weak for this rugged country, and the parts did not seem to fit together as they should.

Ben asked an auto mechanic named Ira Farnsworth to help put the plane together. He also had some willing help from another Fairbanks mechanic named Earl Borland.

"You don't need to pay me," young Borland told him. "I will help you for nothing just to learn how these things are put together. Someday I hope to be a flier, too."

"I'll be glad to teach you. Earl," Ben offered. "Any time."

The long Alaska summer days gave the men plenty of time to work. By the evening of the third day, the Jenny was ready for its first trial flight.

Ira Farnsworth painted FAIRBANKS in big blue letters along the sides of the yellow airplane.

"Now if you get lost, Ben," he said, "people will know where you came from."

Ben smiled, but he felt uneasy. Without knowing it, Ira Farnsworth had touched a tender spot. It would be very easy to get lost in the bush country of Alaska. Ben knew his own weakness for losing his way. He had done it several times before.

That evening a crowd gathered at the ball park.

"Stand back away from the propeller," Ben warned them before starting the engine.

He warmed the engine for a few minutes. Then he

waved to the crowd and pushed the throttle forward. The Jenny started to roll across the rough ground of the ball park.

The engine roared. The plane rolled faster and faster, but it did not lift from the soft ground. There were trees and houses beyond the ball park. The Jenny was headed right for them.

"Come on!" Ben shouted above the roar of the propeller. "Up! Up!"

He pulled back hard on the control stick. The Jenny bounced one last time and rose into the sky. It barely missed the trees.

For the next ten minutes Ben circled over the town. Every place he looked there were hills and streams.

Between them were great spreading plains of flat and rolling tundra. The tundra was covered with hundred of lakes, both large and small. In all directions the country around Fairbanks looked the same.

Ben flew in a circle around the city. Then he made a dive over the ball park. The people ran for cover, as though they thought he was going to crash. Ben pulled out of the dive just above the ground. He circled the ball park once. Then he came back for a landing.

"That's enough for now," he said. "I will save all of my stunts for the big show I will put on tomorrow."

The next day was the Fourth of July, one of the biggest holidays in Alaska. When he got to the ball park, a big crowd was already on hand. There were miners and trappers, merchants and fishermen, Eskimos and Indians.

The crowd kept getting bigger and bigger. More and more tickets were sold. Finally, Ben climbed into the pilot's cockpit.

Ira Farnsworth waved the people back out of the way. He took hold of the propeller and gave it a hard jerk. The engine sputtered and came to life.

Ben picked a smooth path on the baseball field from which to take off. The engine roared. The Jenny raced forward. It bounced a couple of times and took off.

For the next half hour Ben did everything but turn the Jenny inside out. He looped, he dived, he spun the plane all over the sky.

He could not hear the cheers from the crowd looking up at him from the baseball park, but he could tell by the way they waved and ran around that they were excited by the air show.

As a final stunt Ben dived low over the ball park. Then he turned the Jenny over on its back. He flew upside down over the heads of the crowd.

At the far end of the field he flipped the Jenny right side up again. He made a sharp turn and came in for a landing.

The people of Fairbanks had seen their first flying show. They cheered Ben as he shut off the engine and climbed out of the cockpit.

"Hurrah for Ben!"

"Hurrah for the Flying Professor!"

Banker Dick Wood hurried over to the plane. He was waving a piece of paper in his hand. "That was a great show, Ben," he said, smiling, "and look what I have."

"What is it?"

"A telegram from Nenana. They want you to fly down there and put on a show for them."

"Right now?"

"Yes. They are having a Fourth of July celebration there, too. They will pay five hundred dollars if you will put on a show for them."

"Wow!" Ben exclaimed. "That's a lot of money."

"That's right," Dick Wood said, "and our company can use it."

Ben looked at the sky. The sun was still high. It would be daylight for a long time yet. Nenana was only sixty miles away. There was plenty of time to fly there, put on a show, and fly back to Fairbanks again.

"All right, we'll do it," Ben said. "How about your flying to Nenana with me, Dick?"

The banker started to shake his head. He looked at the Jenny. Then he looked at Ben. "Will you be careful, Ben?" he asked.

"Of course."

"Will you land and let me off at Nenana before you start doing all those stunts?"

"If you want me to."

"All right, I'll go with you," Dick Wood said. "Besides, I suppose someone has to show these people that our airplane company also carries passengers."

Dick Wood climbed into the front cockpit. They took off and headed for Nenana.

After a few miles Ben decided to leave the railroad and try taking a shortcut to Nenana. Once he reached the Tanana River, he should have no trouble finding the town.

A half hour passed. He saw a lot of water, but nothing that looked like the Tanana River.

"I should have stuck to the railroad," he thought. "If I run out of gas here, I will crash on the tundra. Why didn't I play it safe?"

Dick Wood pointed off to one side where a tiny cloud of gray smoke was climbing into the sky.

"That must be Nenana," Ben thought. Feeling much better, he turned the airplane. As he flew over, he saw that the smoke came from a lone trapper's cabin. Nenana was still not in sight.

"I'm lost again!" Ben cried into the wind. "Why did I ever try taking a shortcut?"

He knew he could not have much fuel left.

"There's about enough gas to fly one big circle," he said to himself. "Then I will have to make a crash landing."

Ben looked at Dick Wood's back and hoped the banker did not know that they were lost and in trouble.

He turned the airplane slowly in a wide circle. He watched the ground closely as they passed over. Five minutes went by. Ben waited for the last sputter of the engine.

All at once he saw the flash of the sun on railroad tracks, and those tracks led to Nenana. Just as the engine began to sputter, he saw the town straight ahead. With a little luck he could make it.

He flew over the town, trying to pick a place to land. The engine coughed a final time and died. The only sound now was the whistle of the wind through the Jenny's wire braces.

"Ben," Dick called. "Look up ahead. See all those people? It looks like a ball park. It must be where they want us to land."

Ben saw the worry on the banker's face. There was no doubt that for some time Dick Wood had known they were in trouble.

"Can we make it on a dead engine, Ben?"

"We can only try," Ben called back.

He used all his skill to stretch out the glide. They barely missed the last row of cabins. The baseball park was now within reach.

The Jenny hit the ground and bounced high. Ben fought the controls to keep it from turning over. The plane hit again and stayed down.

It was a rough landing. But Ben was beginning to feel that any landing in Alaska that you lived through was a good one.

The people cheered as the Jenny rolled to a stop. Ben just sat for a moment. Then he took off his helmet and goggles. He wiped the sweat from his face and smiled at Dick Wood. The banker smiled weakly back.

Both knew they had just had a close call.

BUSH PILOT
CHAPTER 9

BEN PUT on his air show for the people of Nenana, Then he picked up Dick Wood and flew back to Fairbanks. This time he followed the railroad tracks all the way so he would not get lost.

The people around Fairbanks saw that Dick Wood had come back safely from his airplane ride. Now many others were willing to try it. They came to the ball park with money in their hands. A few of the old sourdoughs even brought gold dust with which to pay for their rides.

For the next few days Ben was kept busy taking people on short hops in the Jenny. Each time he flew a little different way.

"I want to learn this country by heart," he told Wrong Font. "I want to know every landing spot, every turn in the river, every sandbar. Then I won't get lost."

Within a short time all those who wanted rides had taken their turns. There was nothing for the Jenny to do.

"I was afraid this would happen," Ben said. "You can't run an airplane company just doing stunting shows and taking a few people on joy rides around town."

"Don't worry about it, Ben," Wrong Font said. "We have already taken in more than enough money to pay for the Jenny. You are the best flier in all Alaska."

Ben laughed. "Right now I guess I am the *only* flier in Alaska." He ran his fingers through his light, thinning hair. "Wrong Font, we have to do more. We have to show the people that aviation is really needed in Alaska. They must learn that an airplane can answer some of Alaska's worst problems. We won't do any more stunting or joy rides."

"All right," the newspaper editor said, "I agree with you, Ben. Let's hope that we get a chance to show what an airplane can really do here."

A few days later that chance came. Dick Wood rushed out to the ball park where Ben was working on the Jenny's engine.

"Ben, how would you like to fly out to the Stewart and Denhart mine?"

"Where is it?"

"Out on Caribou Creek, about eighty miles from here. They have had a breakdown. They need some new parts to fix their mining machinery."

"If the parts are not too heavy, I can take them," Ben said.

"Good. By the way, Ben, they want you to carry a lawyer up there, too. They need some legal papers written up."

"Fine," Ben said. "Anything else?"

"Just the mail at the post office which has been piling up for a month or more. You know how important mail is to miners."

"Sure," Ben said. "I'll take anything they want so long as it's not so heavy that I can't get the Jenny off the ground."

The next day Ben flew away with the lawyer, the

machinery parts, and the mail. He took off and flew north toward Caribou Creek.

After about an hour of flying he saw the Stewart and Denhart mine diggings. Nearby was a rough sandbar which the miners had quickly cleared for a landing field. They had done a poor job of it. They had left rocks and stumps right where Ben wanted to land.

He looked around for another place. There was nothing better than the sandbar.

"Hold on," he shouted to the lawyer. "We'll have to try it—rocks, stumps, and all!"

As he glided in for a landing, Ben worked the control stick and rudder pedals hard in order to miss a few of the rocks and stumps. The Jenny hit hard, but held together.

As soon as the plane bounced to a stop, the lawyer climbed out of the cockpit shaking his head. "For a minute I thought we were done for," he said.

"Oh, I've made worse landings than that," Ben said

smiling. "But I wouldn't have had to if those miners had cleared the rocks and stumps off this sandbar."

The mine owners were happy to get the machinery parts so quickly. The miners gathered around eagerly to get their mail.

"How long did it take you to get here in the flying machine?" one of the miners asked Ben.

"Oh, a little over an hour."

"A little over an hour!" one of them exclaimed. "You know how long it takes to get here coming over the trail from Fairbanks?"

"How long?"

"About six days."

Ben smiled. "Well, that just shows you what an airplane can do."

"Eielson," one of the mine owners said, "you can count on plenty of business from us in the future."

"Fine," Ben said. "But first how about fixing up that landing strip? I can't land a plane where there are big rocks and tree stumps."

"Sure. Don't worry. We'll fix it up."

During the following weeks Ben found many jobs for himself and the Jenny.

One day word came to Fairbanks that a miner was very sick far out in the bush country. Ben flew a Fairbanks doctor to the man.

"It was the only way that fellow's life could have been saved, Ben," the doctor told him after he had treated the sick man. "Someday I may get an airplane of my own. It would help me to get around to sick people."

Then smallpox struck an Indian village on the Yukon River. Again Ben flew the doctor and medicine to the place.

"We never would have made it in time if I had taken the trail," the doctor said. "Ben, do you know how many lives have been saved already by using this airplane?"

Ben was thinking of something else. If the village had been a few miles farther away from Fairbanks than it was, they never could have reached it in the Jenny.

"This plane is too small," he told Dick Wood one day. "It can carry enough gas for about 150 miles. Alaska's a big territory, Dick. We need a plane that will reach places farther away."

"What do you have in mind, Ben?"

"Well, the army's De Havilland will go twice as far and carry twice as big a load."

"Yes, but how can we get one from the army?"

"I have been writing to Washington," Ben said. "I am trying to get them to let me have a De Havilland to fly airmail up here."

"Any luck?"

"Not so far," Ben said, shaking his head.

"Let's do the best we can with what we have."

"O.K., but winter is not far off, Dick. I don't think the Jenny will be much good for winter flying."

The banker looked surprised. "Ben, I don't think anything will fly up here in the winter. Even the birds don't fly. Why, there is so much ice and snow and sub-zero cold that often even the sled dogs can't move. An airplane? I don't think so, Ben."

"I would still like to try it," Ben said.

The banker looked at his friend. "I bet you would even like to try flying over the North Pole."

"Why not?" Ben said. "It's the shortest way to get to Europe, isn't it? Or from Europe to Asia? All you have to do is to look at a globe to see that."

"It will take better planes than we have now to do it, Ben."

"Someday we will have better planes."

Ben flew the Jenny for a few more weeks, but the weather was getting colder. The Jenny was beginning to wear out as a result of several crash landings Ben had made. Each one had left the airplane in a little worse shape than before. The Jenny began to rattle like a bag full of tin cans.

September came. Ben had been in Alaska just a

year. Once again the ice began to form on the Chena River. The skies turned gray. The nights grew long. Heavy fog often lay like a dark blanket over the town. All in all it was poor weather for flying. "Ben," Ira Farnsworth said, "I guess it's about time for you to put the Jenny away and go back to teaching school."

Ben had already made up his mind to do something else. During the summer he had begun to see what airplanes could do for Alaska.

"I am not going back to teaching school, Ira," he said.

"You're not? Then what are you going to do all winter, Ben?"

"I hope to keep on flying."

"What in? Not the Jenny, I hope. It's about ready to fall apart, Ben. I can't do much more to keep it together."

"You're right about the Jenny, Ira," Ben said. "But I have other plans. Cross your fingers and hope they work out."

"My fingers are crossed, Ben. Good luck! You'll need it if you hope to fly in the winter up here—and stay alive."

Ben smiled, but he had made up his mind.

He knew that Ira Farnsworth spoke the truth. Flying in the wintertime in Alaska could be a dangerous game.

AIRMAIL
CHAPTER 10

With Dan Sutherland's help, Ben got an airmail contract from the Post Office Department in Washington, D.C. The contract called for ten round-trip flights between Fairbanks and the town of McGrath, about three hundred miles away.

It was a trial contract. If everything went all right, he could keep the airmail contract. If things went badly, however, the government would end the contract and stop the flights.

The government also shipped an army De Havilland airplane to Fairbanks for Ben to use.

"Just remember, Ben," Dan Sutherland wrote from Washington, "the dog-team drivers and the riverboatmen have been carrying the mail in Alaska for many years. They are not going to like the idea of losing their jobs to an airplane pilot."

"I don't like to take the jobs away from the dog mushers and the boatmen," Ben told Ira Farnsworth. "But if we always stuck to the old ways of doing things, how could America ever grow better?"

"You're right, Ben," his friend said. "Sometimes those dogsleds take three weeks to make the round trip to McGrath. You should be able to do it in the De Havilland in a few hours."

"That's right," Ben said.

The winter snows lay deep on the ground. The arctic air was biting cold. The lakes and streams were frozen over.

With the help of a carpenter, Ben made a giant pair of skis. He took the wheels off the airplane and put the skis on.

"The skis will be much better for taking off and landing on ice and snow," Ben said.

Ira Farnsworth said, "You will have to be careful. No one ever has flown in Alaska in the winter. Your engine may freeze up. Heavy ice may form on the wings and force you down. The De Havilland may not be able to get over some of the high mountains. If you get caught in a storm, you may never get out of it alive."

Ben knew all of this. Still he was willing to try it.

On the dark cold morning of February 21, 1924, he went to the ball park. He was dressed in a fur coat, bearskin mittens, and fur-lined boots, but the freezing air bit into him.

A crowd of people had gathered to see him begin Alaska's first airmail flight. Soon the mail was loaded in the plane.

Ira Farnsworth stored some food, a pair of snowshoes, a gun, and an ax in with the mail.

"If you are forced down, Ben," he said, "those things might help save your life."

"Thanks, Ira. I hope I don't have to use them."

Ben warmed up the engine. It roared louder than the old Jenny's. It was a more powerful engine. The De Havilland was a much bigger and heavier airplane than the Jenny had been.

By the time Ben had checked everything and was ready to take off, the skis had frozen fast to the snow.

"Help me rock the plane to break them loose," Ben called to the group of men standing nearby.

They pushed and pulled. They rocked the De Havilland's wings. Finally the skis broke loose from the snow.

Ben pushed the throttle forward, the airplane roared, and the skis skidded across the snow. Then the plane rose into the air.

Ben circled Fairbanks once. He waved as he flew over the ball park. Then he pointed the plane's nose toward the Tanana River.

He looked down at the snow-covered land. It looked the same in all directions.

"I must be careful not to get lost," he warned himself.

Less than an hour later he flew over Nenana. There he turned and flew south until he saw the dogsled trail in the snow below him. He flew low to keep the sled tracks in sight.

When he saw a large frozen lake below the De Havilland's wings, he checked his map and thought, "That's Lake Minchumina! Already I'm more than halfway to McGrath."

There were some small dark spots moving slowly across the ice. He dived low to get a better look. What he saw was the dog team and sled carrying the mail that had left Fairbanks over a week ago.

"He still has over a hundred miles to go before he reaches McGrath," Ben thought.

As he roared past, Ben waved at the man and dogs staring up at him. They were quickly left behind.

Three hours and nine minutes after he left Fairbanks, Ben brought the De Havilland to a skidding stop on the frozen river at McGrath.

The crowd shouted a welcome and rushed across the ice to greet Ben.

"Hurrah for Ben Eielson!" they shouted.

Ben grinned happily. The first time that anyone tried to deliver mail by airplane in Alaska was a big success.

But Ben knew the dim winter daylight would not last long. He wanted to fill up the gas tanks and head back to Fairbanks while there was still enough light to see his way.

The people of McGrath did not want him to go. They bad planned a party in his honor. He did not want to hurt their feelings by not going to his own party. He only hoped it would be short.

It was not. By the time everyone had finished eating and the speeches were over, it was growing dark again.

Ben hurried back to the plane. He got one of the men to spin the propeller for him. He climbed in and

waved to the crowd. After three tries the engine started. Soon Ben was back in the air.

In the dim light it was hard to make out where he was. Now and then he stuck his head out over the edge of the cockpit to look down, but he quickly ducked back in as the icy wind stung his face.

"It all looks the same down there," he said to himself. "I hope that I am on my course."

Then he looked down and saw the frozen Lake Minchumina again. The dog team still had not reached the end of the lake.

This time Ben did not dive down to wave at the dog-team musher. The sky was filling with fog and clouds, and he was only halfway home. Darkness came quickly as the De Havilland flew into the clouds.

Ben looked at his compass. It was acting strangely. The needle was swinging back and forth. A sudden fear gripped Ben.

"No, no!" he shouted into the wind. "Not now! I mustn't get lost now!"

He flew on and on, through clouds and fog and darkness. He kept looking at his watch. He hoped he had been staying on his course.

"I should be nearly to Fairbanks by now," he said. "But I can't see the ground. Oh, why did I stay for that party at McGrath? I should have started back while it was still daylight and the weather was good."

He looked at his gas gauge. There was very little fuel left in the tanks. Looking out, he saw a coat of ice forming on the leading edges of the wings.

"If it gets much thicker, it will make the plane too heavy," he thought, "and I will crash."

Now and then a chunk of ice broke loose and banged against the plane. One piece smashed through the cloth covering.

"If only I could find a break in the clouds," he said to himself hopefully, "I might be able to see the lights of Fairbanks."

There was no break. He was almost sure that he would have to make a crash landing.

Suddenly, he saw a faint glow of light pushing up through the clouds. He turned toward it. The clouds opened up. Below him was a light, in fact, a row of lights!

"What can they be?" Ben wondered, staring through his goggles. Then he knew.

"They are bonfires!" he shouted into the wind. "The people have lighted bonfires to help me get home!"

He pulled back on the throttle and glided through the darkness. He lined the plane up with the row of bonfires.

"Which side of them do I land on?" he wondered. "I can't see the ground. I can see only the fires. Where is the landing strip?"

He had to take a chance. He cut the engine. The cold wind whistled through the wing braces.

At the last moment he saw the field, but he was off to one side of the landing strip.

He tried to turn the plane. He was too low. One ski caught in a treetop. The De Havilland dropped and hit the ground hard. As the ski broke, the plane nosed over, smashing its propeller. The De Havilland skidded across the icy ground. It tipped up and came to rest on its nose.

Ben was shaken. He sat in the cockpit wondering whether he was still in one piece. He heard people shouting and running toward him across the frozen snow.

Then gentle hands were helping to lift him out of the cockpit.

"What are you grinning about, Ben?" someone asked.

"Am I grinning?" Ben asked. Yet he knew he was, and he knew the reason for it.

He had lived through the first round-trip airmail flight ever made in Alaska. He had shown it could be done, and that was something to grin about.

ON SILVER WINGS
CHAPTER 11

SINCE THE day he made his first flight over Fairbanks in the old Jenny, Ben had been well known all over Alaska. Now, as the pioneer country's first airmail pilot he was the bush country hero.

Wrong Font Thompson wrote a glowing report in the *News-Miner*.

Ben wrote a simpler report to the Post Office Department in Washington.

One day a letter came to him from the President of the United States, Calvin Coolidge. It told him what a fine job he had done.

"Ben," said Dick Wood, "Alaska has never had a hero like you. We've needed one."

Ben smiled. Being a hero meant very little to him. "I am up here to do a job, Dick," he said. "To prove what airplanes can do for Alaska is what really counts."

Ben went on flying the mail between Fairbanks and McGrath. His next three trips were made without trouble.

By April much of the snow was gone. The ice had broken up on the lakes and rivers. Ben took off the skis from the De Havilland and put on the wheels again.

Soon the frozen ground thawed and turned soft and muddy. While landing after the fifth trip to McGrath, the wheels of the plane sank into the ground. The De Havilland flipped over on its back, smashing the propeller and wings.

Ben had to wait for new parts to be sent from the States.

A warning letter from the Post Office Department asked him to be more careful with the De Havilland, which was owned by the government.

Ira Farnsworth laughed when Ben showed him the letter. "They don't know how lucky they are that the plane isn't smashed up every time you land," he said. "They can have no idea how tough it is to fly up here and stay in one piece."

"It will get easier, Ira," Ben said. "One day Alaska will be full of airplanes, and we'll have radio and other things to help us find our way around. We'll fly through snow, fog, hail, or rain as though it wasn't there. You'll see."

In the meantime, Ben had to fly without the help of radio or other aids to a pilot.

On his sixth trip to McGrath, Ben landed to find a group of miners waiting for him.

"Ben," their leader said, "one of our men is very sick. He needs to be taken to the Fairbanks Hospital right away. Will you do it?"

"I'm sorry," Ben said, "but a government rule won't allow me to carry a passenger in a mail plane. I'm afraid you'll have to take him to Fairbanks by dogsled."

"That would take weeks, Ben. He would never live through it."

Ben looked at the sick man, an old sourdough. He seemed to be in bad shape. Rules were rules, but there was a man's life to think about.

Ben turned to the other miners. "I am going to be gone for a few minutes," he said. "When I get back, I won't know whether or not that man has been put in with the mailbags and tied in well."

The miners did not say anything, but their eyes sparkled. Ben turned and walked away.

A few minutes later he took off for the return trip to Fairbanks. He hoped his unseen passenger was comfortable in among the mailbags—that is, if he was up there at all. Ben was not sure. He had not looked.

As he came in for a landing at Fairbanks, the De

Havilland's wheels hit a soft spot in the runway. The plane skidded around, hit a ditch, and flipped over.

Hanging upside down, Ben quickly unhooked his safety belt and fell to the ground. He crawled under the plane to the place where the mail was stored. The old sourdough hung upside down in his safety belt. Ben unhooked the belt and lowered the sick miner gently to the ground.

The man looked up at him and shook his head. "Ben," he said, "is that the way you always land a plane?"

Seeing that the man was not hurt, Ben laughed. "Well, not always," he said. "Not always."

The airplane was in bad shape. Once again Ben had to send to the States for some new parts. In time the parts arrived as well as another warning letter telling him to be more careful in the future.

"They must think you are cracking this plane up for the fun of it," Ira Farnsworth said.

When the plane was fixed again, Ben made his seventh mail trip. Everything went well. Ben was being very careful. Just three more flights would finish up the contract. If nothing happened to wreck the plane, he was almost sure to get a new contract. It would mean he had really proved the worth of airmail in Alaska.

He even hoped the government would give him

more airplanes. With more planes and pilots new airmail routes could be set up to cover many parts of Alaska.

Ben knew he could train men as pilots. Earl Borland had often said that he would like to be a flier, and there were others who felt the same. But Ben had hoped ahead of time.

On the eighth flight the weather was warm and rainy. As he landed at Fairbanks, one wheel hit a mudhole. The De Havilland spun across the ground and tipped over on its back.

Once again Ben unhooked his safety belt and dropped to the ground. Luckily he was not hurt, but the plane was a wreck.

"Maybe I gave the sick sourdough the wrong answer that day," he said looking at the broken propeller and smashed wings. "I guess I do always land this way."

Ben sent a telegram to the Post Office Department asking for some more new parts for the plane. Within two days he got a telegram in reply. As he read it, his heart sank. The government had given up the contract. The airmail must stop.

The Post Office Department felt that the number of wrecks Ben had had with the government plane proved that it was too risky to deliver mail by airplane in Alaska. He was told to ship what was left of the De Havilland back to the States.

Even Dan Sutherland in Washington could not get the government to change its mind.

Everyone in Alaska thought the airmail had been a great success. Ben had proved that a plane could fly in rain or sunshine, in blizzards and in fog, in hot weather and in sub-zero weather.

He had not lost or failed to deliver a single letter or package sent by plane. Still, the mail contract went back to the dog mushers and the riverboatmen.

Ben was without a job and without an airplane. People tried to cheer him up.

"You did a great job, Ben."

"Don't worry, Ben. Soon the airmail will be flying again in Alaska. Just wait and see."

Ben waited a little while. A few other airplanes had arrived in Fairbanks during the months he was delivering mail. Now he became a pilot for one of these new companies.

For a few weeks he flew back and forth into the bush. One day he would carry a miner to a distant gold mine. The next day he might haul a trapper and his dogs to one end of a trapline. A week of so later he would fly out and pick them up again at the far end of the trapline.

He flew medicine to the Indians and Eskimos. He carried sick or injured people to the Fairbanks Hospital. He hauled food and machinery.

This kind of bush flying always excited him. Something new happened every day. It was always dangerous, always interesting. But it was not what Ben really wanted to do.

One day he bought a ticket, got on the train, and headed back to Hatton.

CLIPPED WINGS
CHAPTER 12

HIS FAMILY in Hatton was happy to see him. But not being around airplanes made Ben feel like a bird with its wings clipped. He was too restless to sleep. Night after night he paced back and forth in his room.

"Ben, why don't you go back to school?" Elma asked one day. "You could still be a fine lawyer."

"Elma is right," his father said hopefully. "Give up the flying, Ben. I still think flying is only for birds, not for men. Besides, what have these years of flying done for you, Son? Most of your luck with airplanes has been bad, it seems."

Ben knew this was true. His father was wise, but there were things his father might not understand.

How could Ben put the thrill of flying high above the clouds into words that his father would understand? How could he explain to a man who had never flown the wonders of looking down upon the earth from far above? Even more than that, how could he explain his interest in the future of aviation to a man who thought of airplanes as death traps?

Maybe both Elma and his father were right, Ben thought. He had been flying for years now. What did he really have to show for it? So Ben got on the train that would take him east again to Georgetown University.

On the train he bought a newspaper. One story caught his eye. It told of an Australian explorer named Captain George Hubert Wilkins.

Years ago Captain Wilkins had traveled the arctic regions with the well known explorer Vilhjalmur Stefansson. They had used dog teams.

Now in the newspaper story Captain Wilkins said he believed the arctic could best be explored by airplane.

"I agree," Ben said to himself. "I certainly do agree! Good luck to him!"

Ben returned to his classes at Georgetown University, but he had a hard time keeping his mind on the lessons. Several times he went into town to talk with his friend Dan Sutherland.

"Can't we do anything about getting a new airmail contract for Alaska, Mr. Sutherland?" he asked.

The older man looked at him. "Ben, I thought you had given up flying. I thought you were here to finish law school."

Ben smiled. "I guess that's right. But if the government would give me another airmail contract for Alaska, I might change my mind."

"Still want to fly, Ben?"

"Yes, sir."

"Well, I'm afraid the airmail contract is out. I learned just the other day that new contracts have been given to the dog-team drivers. You'd better stick to law school, Ben."

Ben tried to take his friend's words to heart, but his mind was too much on flying. He could think of little else. He fell behind in his studies, and after three weeks he dropped out of school. He joined the Army Air Service.

During his year in the Air Service, Ben talked to everyone who would listen to him about how important airplanes could be to Alaska. Some people agreed. Some did not. No one did anything about it.

"It looks as though I'll have to prove it myself," Ben said.

This might not be easy. Ben had no idea how he would get back to Alaska to do more flying.

In the meantime the Army Air Service allowed him to build and test new airplane skis.

"They must be lighter and stronger," Ben told the men who worked with him. "Heavy skis can keep a plane from being able to take off. Weak skis can break up on a hard landing and kill the bush pilot."

"Bush pilot?" one of his friends said. "Ben, you are in the Air Service now. You're not flying over the Alaska bush country."

Ben smiled. "Sorry, I forgot."

"No, you didn't, not really. I don't believe you could ever forget Alaska, not the way you talk about it every chance you get. What you can see in that frozen country is beyond me."

Ben did not try to explain. Unless a person had been to Alaska, there was no point in trying to make him understand it. Unless he had seen and felt the pioneer spirit of the people, a man could not share their hopes, joys, and hardships.

Unless it was in his heart to do so, no one could become a part of such a raw new country. All of these things Ben knew.

In September, 1925, Ben's term in the Army Air Service ended. Once again he returned home to Hatton. Once again everyone was glad to have him back. Once again he had good times with his family. Yet there was still a big gap in his life.

Ben shook the thoughts from his head. "I must quit thinking of flying. After all, I am twenty-eight years old. I have little to show for it. I must settle down and get into some kind of business. I must forget airplanes and flying."

Ben took a job as a salesman. For two months he traveled from town to town, from state to state. He was not a good salesman, and he knew why.

"My heart just isn't in it," he told himself. "But I am trying hard. Perhaps one of these days the Lord will show me a better way." Ben prayed that this would come to pass.

One day his job took him to the northern part of the state. It was evening. Ben was waiting to get his hair cut in the barbershop. The telephone rang.

"Ben," the barber said, "this call is for you."

"For me?"

"You're Ben Eielson, aren't you?"

"Right."

"Then it's for you. It's long distance from Hatton."

Ben hurried to the phone.

"Ben," Ole Eielson shouted at the far end of the line, "I have been calling all over trying to find you."

Ben laughed. "With the little hair I have left," he said, "I guess the barbershop is about the last place you would think of, Dad. What's up?"

"There is a telegram here for you. Son. It's from New York."

"New York? I don't know anyone in New York. Who is it from?"

"A very well known man, Ben."

"Don't keep me guessing. Dad."

"It's from the explorer Vilhjalmur Stefansson."

Ben drew in his breath sharply. Why would he be getting a telegram from Stefansson?

"Please tell me what it says, Dad."

"Well, it's very simple, Ben. A fellow named George Hubert Wilkins is looking for a pilot to take him on some airplane trips into the arctic. Mr. Stefansson told him you might be the right man for the job."

Ben could not believe his ears. He asked his father to read the telegram a second time. There was no mistake. Mr. Stefansson must have heard about his flights in Alaska and thought of him as a pilot for Captain Wilkins.

Ben was very excited. "What do you think of it, Dad?" he asked.

For a while no word was spoken on the other end

of the line. "Ben, you're a grown man," Ole Eielson said finally. "It is not for me to say whether I like the idea or not. You have your own life to lead, Son."

"I'll try to do the right thing, Dad."

"I know you will, Ben. When you make up your mind, call Captain Wilkins." He gave the name of the hotel where Captain Wilkins was staying.

Making up his mind was the easiest thing Ben had done for a long time.

The next day he was on the train to New York to meet Captain George Hubert Wilkins.

TROUBLE AT THE START
CHAPTER 13

FROM THE MOMENT they met and shook hands Ben and Captain Wilkins liked each other. The red-haired Australian explorer was about Ben's own size, but he was nine years older than Ben.

His eyes were bright and eager. His clothes were neat but not fancy. His manner was firm and friendly. He spoke without wasting words.

Ben knew at once that here was a man of action. Here was a man who could be trusted to do the right thing at the right time. Here was a man with whom he would be very proud to fly.

Ben wondered how Captain Wilkins felt about him. His mind was soon put at rest.

"Ben," the explorer said after they had talked for a while, "we are going to have to work fast and hard. My plans are to make a flight into the Arctic Blind Spot next spring."

So that was it, Ben thought. The so-called Arctic Blind Spot was the vast icebound polar region, spreading all the way from land's end to the North Pole itself.

A few men had left their tracks on the large arctic ice pack. They had traveled on foot and by dog team. They had known great suffering—frostbite, hunger, snow blindness, sickness, and injury.

"But no one has ever explored the Arctic Blind Spot in an airplane, Ben," Captain Wilkins said.

"That's true, sir," Ben agreed. "In fact, no airplane has ever gone as far north in Alaska as Point Barrow." Ben was thinking of the village of Barrow, sitting near the farthest north tip of Alaska, which stuck out into the Arctic Ocean. He had heard of Barrow, but few people other than the hundred or so Eskimos and a few whites who lived there had seen the town.

Captain Wilkins smiled. "Strange you should speak of Point Barrow, Ben," he said. "I want to make Barrow our base camp from which to hop off on our polar flights. Do you think we can get a plane up to Barrow?"

"We can try, Captain!" Ben was thrilled with the idea. "Of course, we will have to get over or through the Endicott Mountains first. The maps show that they are high and rugged. We will need a good airplane, sir."

"We will have three airplanes, Ben. They are being built right now."

"Three airplanes!" Ben said with surprise.

Then Captain Wilkins told Ben how the expedition was being set up.

A great deal of money was needed for such an exploration. Several rich Detroit men were so much interested that they had agreed to give them the money. So it was being called the Detroit Arctic Expedition.

"We don't have much money to work with, Ben," Captain Wilkins said. "I'm afraid I won't be able to pay you as much as you are worth."

"Captain," Ben said, "I would work for nothing to help prove the worth of airplanes in Alaska and in the polar regions, too."

Ben was surprised to learn that newspaper reporters and many other people would be going to Point Barrow with them.

"I had hoped for a small, simple expedition, Ben," Captain Wilkins said, "but it has suddenly turned into a big thing. The people who put up the money want the world to know what is taking place. I guess they have that right."

Ben also learned that Major Tom Lanphier, a top-ranking Army Air Service flier, would be going along as a pilot, second in charge of the expedition.

"Ben, I would like to have you go to Fairbanks ahead of us to get things ready," Captain Wilkins said. "Get a place ready to keep the planes in. Line up several good mechanics. Get the best, Ben. If we hope to fly across the top of the world to Spitsbergen, our planes will have to be in tiptop shape."

"Spitsbergen?" Ben voiced his surprise. "We are going to fly to Europe?"

Captain Wilkins smiled. "I guess I forgot to tell you that part of my plans, Ben. Yes, if everything goes right on the first few flights, I hope to try the long one."

"But Spitsbergen is about twenty-two hundred miles over the top of the world."

"That's right. Do you like the idea?"

"I do," Ben said happily. "Any globe shows that the shortest route from western America to Europe is over the arctic—over the top of the world."

"Right, Ben. We can blaze a new polar air trail between America and Europe if we can take off from Point Barrow and fly to Spitsbergen."

Ben said, "Let's hope everything goes right."

But things did not go right.

The first blow to the expedition came when one of the three airplanes caught fire and burned in Detroit shortly after it was built.

The expedition still had two airplanes, both Fokkers. They were single-winged airplanes, but different in size. Both had closed cabins instead of open cockpits like the old Jenny and the De Havilland.

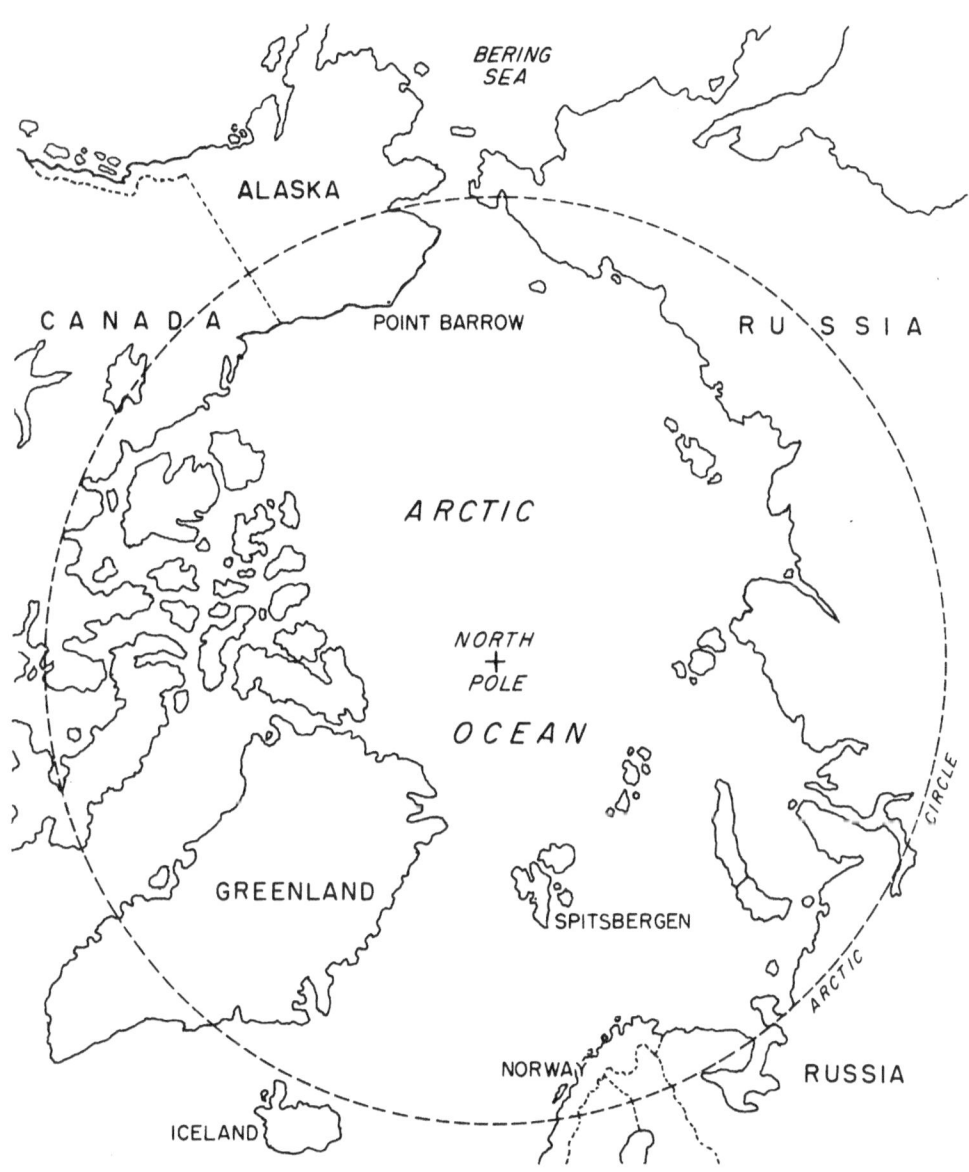

"At least we won't have the icy wind and hail and rain whipping in our faces," Ben thought as he looked over the two airplanes on the Detroit airfield.

The bigger Fokker, named *Detroiter*, had three

powerful engines. The smaller plane with a single engine was named the *Alaskan*.

"You'd better go on to Fairbanks, Ben," Captain Wilkins said. "I'll follow as soon as I can. It will take me a while to get the airplanes ready for shipping and to get the other supplies on the way."

By train and steamer Ben made his way back to Alaska, arriving in Fairbanks on February 17, 1926.

His many friends greeted him happily. Ira Farnsworth and Earl Borland were there to shake his hand.

"It's good to have you back, Ben," Ira said.

"If there is anything I can do to help, Ben," Borland offered, "let me know."

"How are your flying lessons coming along. Earl?" Ben asked.

"Oh, I will never be the world's best pilot, Ben," the cheerful mechanic said. "But I'm learning slowly."

Then Ben heard some bad news. While he had been away, Wrong Font Thompson had died. Ben would miss his good friend. No longer would Wrong Font's glowing words in the *News-Miner* tell Alaskans of aviation's progress in the far north.

A week later Captain Wilkins arrived with the two Fokkers. With him were the men and supplies that he needed for the Detroit Arctic Expedition.

"Thanks for getting things ready, Ben," the expedition's

leader said. "You have done a good job. Now we will have to hurry to get the planes put together and ready to fly."

Ben knew the reason for Captain Wilkins' hurry. March and April were the two best months for flying in the arctic. Later during the warm summer, thick fog would rise from the pack ice. Such fog would be a great danger to flying. Still later, during the long nights of an arctic winter, they would be unable to see at all. Yes, March and April were the best months to explore the Arctic Blind Spot.

"The first thing we must do, Ben," Captain Wilkins said, "is to fly gasoline, food, and supplies to Point Barrow."

"That may turn into quite a job, Captain," Ben said. "Point Barrow is five hundred miles north of here."

"That's right. The Endicott Mountains are in between. We must find a way to get over or through them, but that is part of the plan. Barrow will make a good base camp from which we will hop off into the polar regions. We have to get there."

"Oh, I'm sure we can make it," Ben said cheerfully, "just as soon as the planes are put together."

A few days later the two Fokkers were set for their trial flights. The first flight was to be made in the large three-engine *Detroiter*.

On the morning of the flight it was Major Lanphier, not Ben, who walked through the biting sub-zero cold and climbed into the airplane cabin with Captain Wilkins.

Ben stayed on the ground. He felt left out, but tried not to show his feelings.

Newspaper reporters from the United States were in the crowd that had gathered along the snow-covered runway.

"Get back!" Ben called, as the three propellers of the *Detroiter* started spinning.

Someone yelled, "The wheels are sinking in the snow. Let's help push."

"Stay back!" Ben shouted. "Don't get near those propellers! Stay—"

Then it happened.

One of the reporters had failed either to see the propellers or to hear the shouted warnings.

There was a sickening thud. The reporter was slammed to the icy runway. He lay still.

Trouble had struck again.

First an airplane had been lost by fire. Now a man lay dead in the snow. The Detroit Arctic Expedition had not yet put an airplane into the sky.

MORE HARD LUCK
CHAPTER 14

A FEW DAYS later Captain Wilkins decided to try out the *Alaskan*.

"I want you to be pilot today, Ben," he said. "We are leaving the wheels on the *Alaskan*. I think they will be better than skis for landing on the hard-packed snow at Barrow."

"You mean we are going to Barrow today?"

"No, not today. This will be just a trial flight. I want to make sure the plane is ready before we try the long trip to Barrow."

The March weather was forty below zero, but the sky over Fairbanks was clear.

Ben and Captain Wilkins climbed into the closed cabin of the single-engine airplane. Ben warmed the engine. He listened carefully. It was running smoothly. He nodded to Wilkins, who smiled. His lips formed the words, "Let her go, Ben."

Ben shoved the throttle forward. The metal propeller spun faster and faster. The *Alaskan* started rolling down the icy runway. The propeller whipped up a cloud of snow as the plane sped ahead. When the speed was right, Ben pulled back on the control stick. The plane lifted gently into the sky.

"Good job, Ben," Wilkins called. "Good job!"

They flew around for twenty minutes. Everything worked well.

"That's enough for today, Ben," Wilkins shouted. "Let's go back now."

Ben came down over the field at Fairbanks. He lined the nose of the plane up with the runway. As the plane got lower, he pulled back on the throttle to slow the engine.

"This should be easy," he told himself. "This is a good airplane."

Without warning the engine sputtered. The plane started to drop. Ben jammed the throttle forward again, but it was too late.

The *Alaskan* hit the ground hard, breaking the landing gear. The tips of the metal propeller dug into the snow and bent almost double. The plane skidded through a fence, tearing away a wing before it came to rest.

Ben and Captain Wilkins climbed out, shaken but unhurt. The *Alaskan* was badly wrecked. It would be some time before it would fly again.

Captain Wilkins did not blame Ben for the wreck. However, some of the other men did.

"Wilkins never should have made a bush flier the first pilot of this expedition," one of them said.

"Nothing has gone right," another agreed.

"This expedition has a jinx on it," still another added.

Spirits were low among the members of the expedition.

A few days later Major Lanphier and Captain Wilkins took off in the *Detroiter*. Almost the same thing happened. The *Detroiter* crashed while coming in for a landing. Luckily, again, neither the pilot nor Wilkins was hurt.

Now the expedition was in a bad way. The people in Detroit sent Captain Wilkins a telegram, telling him to get new pilots.

"Maybe they are right, Captain," Ben said. "Maybe I am not fit for this job."

"That is foolish talk, Ben," Captain Wilkins replied. "I will not listen to it. Those planes can be fixed, can't they?"

"Yes, sir," Ben said.

"Then we will fix them up and fly them again, and you will be at the controls, Ben. Understand?"

"Yes, sir," Ben said eagerly. Tears made his eyes smart. Knowing that Captain Wilkins had not lost faith in him filled his heart with joy and thanks.

"We'd better hurry," Captain Wilkins said. "I hear that explorer Richard E. Byrd is shipping a plane to

Kings Bay at Spitsbergen. He hopes to fly from there to the North Pole. Captain Roald Amundsen is at Kings Bay now with the dirigible *Norge*. As soon as the weather is clear, he is going to try flying that cigar-shaped gas bag across the North Pole."

Ben shook his head. "It looks as if everyone and his brother is up here in the arctic getting ready to fly over the top of the world."

"Well, it wouldn't really matter to me if they did," Captain Wilkins said. "I'm not trying to set any records, Ben. I am here for other reasons. I am interested in studying the weather. I would like to take soundings to see how deep the ocean is under the arctic ice pack. I am also interested in finding out whether there is land under the arctic ice. Some people think there is land. Others think there is nothing but the Arctic Ocean underneath. I would like to prove it, one way or another."

Then Wilkins went on. "But the people who put up the money for this expedition would like us to be the first to fly to the North Pole. So we will do our best. After all, without their money to help us, we wouldn't even be here."

Ben worked day and night to help get the *Alaskan* fixed. On March 31, 1926, the plane was ready to fly again. After a trial flight, it was loaded with gasoline to be taken to the base camp at Point Barrow.

It was a big load—nearly six thousand pounds. Ben wondered whether the small airplane could carry so much over the high Endicott Mountains, which lay between Fairbanks and Point Barrow.

"The maps show those mountains at the most only about five thousand feet high, Ben," Captain Wilkins said. "We should be able to get over that all right, don't you think?"

"If they are not higher than that, we should have no trouble," Ben answered, "but the maps in this country are not always right."

The takeoff from Fairbanks was smooth. Captain Wilkins was busy keeping track of their course. As Wilkins laid out the route to be followed, Ben put the plane into a gentle climb. He wanted to be as high as possible by the time they reached the Endicott Mountains.

They flew north for over an hour. Captain Wilkins studied his charts and maps. Often he leaned over and shouted orders into Ben's ear. Ben turned the way he was told. Captain Wilkins set the course. Ben enjoyed not having to worry about getting lost.

When they reached the mountains, their maps proved to be wrong.

"Captain," Ben shouted as they came to the mountains looming up high into the sky, "those mountains are twice as high as the maps show!"

"You're right, Ben. Can we climb any higher with this plane?"

"I'll try, sir. We'll have to get over them or turn back."

Ben was able to push the *Alaskan* up to nine thousand feet, but that was as high as the heavily loaded plane would go. It still was not high enough to cross the mountains.

"It's too late to turn back, Ben!" Wilkins shouted suddenly as a peak loomed in their path.

"We may crash!" Ben shouted. He tried to turn the plane. It was so heavy that it was hard to control.

Then he saw a pass through the mountains. It was very narrow. Maybe it was too narrow for the airplane to get through, but he had to try.

"Hold on, Captain!"

He flew straight into the pass. Strong winds rocked the wings. The *Alaskan* nearly slammed into the side of the mountain. Ben fought at the controls, praying to himself as he did so. On each side the wings almost scraped the steep rocky walls.

Captain Wilkins sat watching. Not once did he shout a warning. Not once did he tell Ben what to do.

"He has faith in me," Ben thought. "I can't let him down!"

Suddenly the plane flew out the far side of the pass. Up ahead stretched endless miles of flat frozen tundra.

"You made it!" Captain Wilkins called. There was a broad smile on the explorer's face. "That was real flying, Ben!"

For the next hour and a half they flew over fog and through clouds. Then there was an opening in the fog. Ben saw the village of Barrow off to one side. Captain Wilkins saw it also, but he pointed on ahead.

"Let's keep going for a while, Ben," he shouted. "We have plenty of gas left."

Soon they were out over the rough ice pack of the Arctic Ocean. No man had ever seen this from the air before.

They flew on—eighty miles—a hundred miles.

Then Captain Wilkins tapped Ben on the shoulder. "This is far enough, Ben," he called. "Let's turn back to Barrow."

By now a storm had moved in behind them. They had trouble finding Barrow. Ben began to sweat. "We shouldn't have gone so far out. We should have kept our eyes on the weather."

Finally, as their gas was getting low, they saw the buildings through the wind-whipped snow.

"Thank goodness, Ben," Captain Wilkins yelled above the roar of the engine.

Ben flew low, feeling his way carefully through the blizzard. When the wheels touched down on the hard-packed snow, the plane began to skid. With all his skill Ben worked the rudder pedals and control stick. The airplane straightened out and slowly rolled to a stop.

"Nice going, Ben," Captain Wilkins patted his shoulder. "That proves we can use wheels up here if we want to. They work all right on ice or hard-packed snow."

The two men climbed out of the airplane. They were greeted by a group of white people. There were many Eskimos at Barrow, too, but they stayed well back away from the strange giant bird that had roared down out of the sky.

"There never has been an airplane this far north before," one of the white traders said. "The Eskimos haven't made up their minds yet whether it is good or bad medicine."

Captain Wilkins smiled. "It's good," he said.

It was good, Ben knew. They had just made the first airplane flight from Fairbanks to Barrow. Also they had flown more than a hundred miles over the ice pack of the Arctic Ocean. It was the first time that had been done, too.

This was just the beginning though. The big job was still ahead.

A CLOSE CALL
CHAPTER 15

CAPTAIN WILKINS and Ben made other flights between Fairbanks and Point Barrow. But storms slowed down their plans to explore the ice pack.

One blizzard raged for days. They could only wait at Barrow and hope the weather would clear. When the storm did move on, a thick gray fog rolled in from the frozen arctic sea.

"Ben," Captain Wilkins said, "we'd better not try flying into the Blind Spot in this fog. The weather looks better inland. Let's fly back to Fairbanks once more and pick up another load of gasoline and supplies. We will need them later on anyway."

As soon as they could see to take off, Ben and the expedition leader walked out to the airplane. They were dressed in their fur-lined coats, mittens, and warm boots.

After heating the engine over a stove and pouring hot oil into the engine, Ben was able to get it started. But the wheels stuck in the snow, and the plane would not move. Captain Wilkins jumped to the ground. He grabbed a wheel and rocked it back and forth until he broke it loose from the ice. The plane jerked forward suddenly.

Ben saw a strange look on Wilkins' face as he climbed into the cabin. The explorer merely nodded, then slid into a seat in the cabin behind Ben.

"It's odd that he doesn't come up here and sit," Ben said to himself. But he gave it no more thought. There had been times before when the explorer stayed in the cabin where there was more room to spread out his maps.

Ben took off and flew south toward Fairbanks. Without the heavy load of gasoline and supplies, the *Alaskan* was able to climb high enough to get over the mountains. Captain Wilkins had not shouted any orders in his ear or passed Ben a single note since they had taken off.

"We must be right on course," Ben told himself.

But a few minutes later Captain Wilkins leaned forward and passed a note over Ben's shoulder.

"Where are we?" the note asked. The words were hard to read, not at all like Wilkins' clear writing.

Ben turned in his seat. He saw a strange pained look on the explorer's face. Something was wrong. A chill passed along Ben's spine.

"I—I must have passed out for a while, Ben," Captain Wilkins yelled above the roar of the engine. "I caught my arm in the wheel back at Barrow. I think I broke it. Do you have any idea where we are?"

"No, sir," Ben said honestly. "I thought we were on course. I didn't know you were hurt, or—"

"It wasn't your doing, Ben," Wilkins said in a voice full of pain. "I wonder whether we can spot anything that will help us find our way?"

They flew over the frozen tundra and winding ice-crusted rivers and creeks.

"Everything looks the same from the air," Ben called. He studied the gas gauge. "We are getting low on gas. If we don't find out where we are pretty quick, we will have to make a crash landing."

Captain Wilkins leaned over his shoulder and pointed out the window. "Isn't that a small village down there, Ben? Let's have a look."

Ben pointed the *Alaskan's* nose toward a cluster of cabins beside the frozen river.

"Fly low, Ben," Wilkins called, "I'll drop them a note."

Ben circled the village. Tiny figures rushed out of

the cabins. They stood in the snow and stared up at the airplane.

"It may be the first airplane they have ever seen," Ben thought.

Painfully Captain Wilkins wrote something on a piece of paper. He showed the roughly written note to Ben.

WHICH WAY TO FAIRBANKS?

With a piece of string they tied the note to a can of food that they had brought along for lunch.

As they flew low over the village, Wilkins dropped the note out a side window. Ben flew in a wide circle. He watched the paper drop to the ground. He saw a man running toward it.

As Ben made another circle of the village, the people hurried around in the snow.

"Look at that, Ben!" Captain Wilkins shouted as they flew over the village for the third time.

Looking down, Ben saw a strange but welcome sight. The people had lined up to form a human arrow. Their dark clothes stood out sharply against the white snow.

"Go the way that arrow is pointing, Ben," Captain Wilkins yelled happily.

As he turned, Ben waved at the villagers in the snow. They waved back.

Less than an hour later Ben brought the *Alaskan* in for a safe landing at Fairbanks.

It had been a close call.

TOO LATE
CHAPTER 16

THE WEATHER in the far north grew worse. Captain Wilkins' arm no longer bothered him, but fog and storms kept him from trying a flight into the Arctic Blind Spot.

The weather was not so bad south of Barrow, however. Ben and Captain Wilkins made two more flights between Fairbanks and Barrow and brought more gasoline and supplies to the northern base camp. The wrecked *Detroiter* had been fixed. Major Lanphier had doubts that the larger three-engine airplane could make the long flight from Fairbanks to Barrow without stopping somewhere for gas. But there was no place between the two settlements where they could get gas.

"We will have to keep using the *Alaskan*, Ben," Captain Wilkins said as they filled the cabin with large cans of gasoline to take to Barrow.

The many flights through storms had been hard on the single-engine Fokker. The rough landings and heavy loads had weakened the aging aircraft.

As the plane raced down the runway at Fairbanks, one wheel hit a bump. Ben and Wilkins were thrown against their safety belts. Ben kept a firm grip on the control stick. But that did little good. They hit a ditch. One of the *Alaskan's* wings snapped off. It folded back and dug into the ground. The plane skidded around in a circle. Then it tipped up on its nose and came to rest.

The cans of gas broke loose and crashed forward in the cabin. One sprang a leak. A strong smell of gasoline filled the cabin.

"Let's get out of here," Ben yelled. "She might catch fire!"

"You get out, Ben!" Wilkins shouted. "I'm pinned down by gas cans. I'm jammed in tight. Get out while there's time!"

"Not without you."

Quickly Ben worked his way into the small space next to the explorer. He grabbed the heavy cans—lifting, pulling, pushing them out of the way. Little by little he could see more of Captain Wilkins beneath the heavy cans of gas.

"Get out, Ben!" Wilkins said painfully. "If she catches fire, she'll explode."

But Ben kept working at the heavy, jammed-in cans. Then he was able to reach into the small space and get his hand on Wilkins' safety belt. He jerked hard and felt it come free.

Wilkins slid quickly out of the seat. Together they forced the cabin door open and jumped to the ground.

"Thanks for the help, Ben," Captain Wilkins said simply. The warm look in his eyes and the firm feel of his hand on Ben's shoulder spoke greater thanks than words.

"We'd better thank the Lord that the gas didn't catch fire," Ben said.

They looked at the *Alaskan* resting on its folded wing.

"I'm afraid she has flown for the last time," Captain Wilkins said. "She is hardly worth fixing up again."

Ben did not answer, but the explorer was right. The *Alaskan* would fly no more.

A few days later Captain Wilkins filled the tanks in the *Detroiter* and took off for Barrow with Major Lanphier as pilot. Ben stayed in Fairbanks.

The *Detroiter* reached Barrow safely, but the fog still covered much of the Arctic Blind Spot. The *Detroiter* had to stay on the ground at Barrow, pinned down by the thick gray mist.

April ended and May arrived. The so-called "best"

flying season was past. It had been anything but good. Still Captain Wilkins was not ready to give up.

"If the weather would just give us a break," he said hopefully, "we might still succeed."

Then, word arrived at Barrow that on May 9, 1926, Richard E. Byrd had flown his three-engine monoplane from Kings Bay, Spitsbergen, to the North Pole. He had circled around the Pole several times, then flown back to Kings Bay. Thus, Byrd became the first person to fly to the top of the world.

A few days later the great Norwegian explorer, Roald Amundsen, also flew across the North Pole in the large dirigible *Norge*. The *Norge* circled the Pole, then flew on south, landing at Teller, Alaska, 2700 miles from Kings Bay.

It had not been Captain Wilkins' idea to set records. Yet the men with money in Detroit had hoped the expedition would earn some glory.

From the very beginning many things had gone wrong with the Detroit Arctic Expedition. Now Richard E. Byrd and Roald Amundsen had won the air race to the Pole.

As though to close the show for the season, a heavy fog hung over the northland. The hope for good flying weather was gone.

The first Detroit Arctic Expedition had come to an end. Captain Wilkins, Ben, and the other men packed up and returned to the United States.

"Don't worry, Ben. We haven't given up," Captain Wilkins said. "If I can get a new plane, I want to come back next year and try again. Would you be my pilot?" Ben looked at this man who did not know the word "quit."

"I'll be ready any time you want me. Captain Wilkins," he said. "Any time!"

A SECOND TRY
CHAPTER 17

LATE IN THE YEAR Ben heard again from Captain Wilkins. The explorer had good news. He somehow had been able to get more money and new airplanes for a second Detroit Arctic Expedition.

In February, 1927, Ben, Captain Wilkins, and other members of the new expedition arrived in Fairbanks. This time they had two Stinson airplanes in which to do their flying. The Stinsons were small biplanes with two sets of wings instead of one. Also they were fitted with strong skis.

"I think these planes will be better for our job than the heavier Fokkers," Captain Wilkins explained to Ben. "I didn't bring another pilot though. Do you happen to know a good bush flier around here? He would be a spare pilot in case we need him."

Ben thought at once of his good friend Joe Crosson. Crosson was a big, dark-haired, cheerful man. He was a fine pilot who knew the Alaska bush country well. Like Ben, he believed firmly that aviation would someday answer Alaska's big travel problem. Joe signed on with the expedition.

During the month of March the two airplanes made several trips hauling men and supplies to Barrow.

"At least we have most of the gasoline that we hauled up here last year and didn't use," Captain Wilkins said. "Now if the weather will give us a break, we will do what we were unable to do last year. We will head into the Arctic Blind Spot."

For days, though, the weather did not clear. It stayed stormy and cold.

Then a break came. On March 29, although the cold stayed at forty degrees below zero, the sky cleared enough to try a take-off.

The single-engine Stinson was filled with gas. Ben and Wilkins were dressed in warm arctic clothing, heavy bearskin mittens, and fur-lined Eskimo boots.

"It might be warm enough in the plane's cabin without them, Ben," Captain Wilkins said. "But if we should be forced down on the polar ice, these clothes could save our lives."

Ben knew his friend was right. In case of trouble they also took two sleeping bags, two pairs of snowshoes, food, and a small radio.

The Stinson roared into the sky from the icy runway at Barrow. Ben pointed its nose northward over the Arctic Ocean.

Beneath them great fields of floating ice drifted past the wings. Ben could see a few smooth patches, but most of the pack ice was very rough and broken. Great force from the churning sea had stacked the ice into a jumble of sharp ridges. Here and there the ice pack had parted. Dark strips of ocean water called leads cut jagged paths through the floating ice pans.

They flew on for several hours.

Captain Wilkins shouted, "Ben, we are looking down on a part of the world that man has never seen before."

"I'm glad we are up here, Captain," Ben called back. "It doesn't look too friendly down there."

"I wonder how deep that water is," Wilkins said. "I would like to take some soundings."

The only way to take soundings, Ben knew, was to land, and he certainly hoped he would not have to land on that jumble of broken ice beneath them.

Five minutes later the Stinson's engine began to sputter and miss. Ben shot a worried look over at his friend.

The explorer called, pointing down, "There's an ice pan below us that looks big enough and smooth enough to land on. We'd better go down and try to fix the engine."

Ben nodded. They could never hope to make it

back to Point Barrow with the engine acting as it was. He cut the throttle and glided down toward the smoothest patch of ice he could see.

Down! Down! The wind whistled through the wing braces.

A sharp ridge of ice loomed ahead of them. Ben jerked back on the stick. The Stinson barely missed the ridge, then dropped onto the smooth ice beyond.

"That was a great landing," Captain Wilkins said as the plane skidded to a stop. "You have proved that a safe landing can be made out here on the arctic ice pack. It's the first time it's ever been done."

But Ben was thinking about the engine.

"While you see what's wrong," Wilkins said, "I'm going to take a sounding to see how deep the ocean is out here."

Ben wanted to say something, but he did not. They had a dead engine in their airplane. The cold was about forty degrees below zero. In the distance storm clouds were gathering. Maybe he would be unable to fix the engine.

However, Captain Wilkins did not seem worried. He was going to take soundings in order to find out how deep the Arctic Ocean was at that point! He took some instruments from the plane and walked out of sight beyond a ridge of ice.

Ben took off his mittens and started to work on the engine. Soon his fingers were numb with cold.

Ben found what was wrong with the engine. By the time Captain Wilkins returned to the airplane, Ben had it ready to go.

"Ben," Wilkins cried, "the ocean beneath us is three miles deep!"

"Three miles deep!" Ben exclaimed. "Wow!"

"It's the deepest water ever found in the arctic."

"Is that good. Captain?"

"Good? I'll say it's good, Ben. It may mean that there is no land underneath the polar ice. That's not real proof, of course. There could be land farther north toward the Pole. But for years men have wondered whether the arctic ice pack rested on land or floated on top of the ocean. This may help us to find the answer."

"Captain," Ben said, looking toward the heavy storm clouds, "hadn't we better start back to Barrow? If we have any more engine trouble, or if we get caught in that storm—"

"Yes, yes, you're right. Let's go."

Ben pulled the plane into the air just before they reached an open lead in the ice. About ten minutes later the engine began to sputter again.

Once more Ben was able to find a level patch of ice

and land safely. Once more he took off his mittens and worked on the engine until it ran smoothly.

As he climbed back into the airplane, the fingers of his right hand hurt badly. They had turned white. He was sure they were frozen. There was no time, though, to worry about that. The storm had moved in around them. Ben saw with alarm that his fuel was getting low. He did not say anything about his frozen fingers to captain Wilkins.

"Strong winds have been robbing us of fuel," he said. "We will be lucky if we can make it back to Barrow."

The captain answered, "We've got to make it. It's important that the world knows the results of our soundings."

Ben smiled. It was just like the brave explorer to worry more about how deep the Arctic Ocean was than about his own safety.

Using all his skill, Ben got the Stinson back into the air. The engine still did not sound just right. The needle of the gas gauge dropped steadily toward EMPTY.

Ben tried to climb above the storm. But the plane could not make it. Darkness came. Wind, snow, and ice slammed against the Stinson. The plane pitched up and down. Ben feared the wings might break off at any moment. Yet the strong little plane flew on for nearly an hour.

"We're less than a hundred miles from Barrow now, Ben," Captain Wilkins shouted above the howling of the storm and the roar of the engine. "How is our gas holding out?"

Ben did not have time to answer as the engine sputtered and died. Now there was only the shriek of the wind around them.

"That's it!" Ben called.

Darkness was around him. The ice below was a faint gray color. Ben could not see it well enough to tell whether it was smooth or rough.

"I can't see anything below," Wilkins shouted. "Can you?"

"No, sir," Ben answered. He gripped the control stick firmly. "I'll have to make a blind landing."

"Good luck, Ben. Good luck!"

"Brace yourself. We're going down!"

STORMBOUND
CHAPTER 18

BEN SAW the ice just in time to level off the plane, but it was rough, jumbled ice. The Stinson hit hard. A ski broke. A wing dug into an ice ridge and crumpled.

Ben closed his eyes. There was no more that he could do. The plane skidded and bounced. It finally came to a jarring rest up against a snowbank.

Ben opened his eyes and looked around in the darkness of the cabin. Wilkins' seat belt had broken. He was just picking himself up from the floor.

"Are you hurt. Captain?" Ben called.

"Just shaken up. What about you, Ben?"

"Nothing broken. Nothing but the airplane, that is."

The two men climbed out to see in the dark how badly the Stinson was damaged. The raging storm quickly drove them back into the cabin, but they had seen enough.

"This plane will never fly again," the explorer said, "even if we had more gas. It's too badly wrecked."

"I agree." Ben said.

"Well, that leaves just one thing for us to think about, doesn't it, Ben?"

"Yes, sir. It is going to be a long cold hike back to Barrow."

Ben did not add that they stood a good chance of not even making it, nor did Captain Wilkins. The thought was there in the dark cabin of the wrecked Stinson, however. Few men had lived through such a walk across the arctic ice as lay ahead of them.

"There is nothing we can do while this storm keeps up," Wilkins said. He reached for one of the sleeping bags. "We'd better get some sleep. We will need all the rest we can get before we start our long hike."

For five days and nights the storm raged. The wind howled. It rocked the plane and piled snow up against it.

The floating ice moved and groaned beneath them. Ben hoped the pack would not suddenly open up and drop them into the churning sea.

The two men ate a little of their small supply of food.

Three of the four fingers that Ben had frozen while working on the engine were paining him. The fourth one, the little finger on his right hand, had no feeling at all, and it was turning black.

"That finger is in bad shape, Ben," Captain Wilkins

said. "We must get you to a doctor somehow before poison sets in."

Several times they tried to send word out on their small radio. It was not working right. They had little hope that its weak signal would reach through the raging storm to Barrow.

Captain Wilkins wrote the story of their flight on the wall of the Stinson's cabin.

"That's in case this plane is ever found," he explained, "and we are not. At least people will know what happened. They will know the results of our soundings. I'm sorry I got you into this."

"Well, I'm not, Captain," Ben said. "I am here because I wanted to be. It was my own free choice. I knew the chances I was taking. And that is the way I wanted it."

"You are a real man, Ben."

"If I am, that makes two of us. Captain. Real cold men, I might add."

They laughed. The mist from their breath froze on the sides of the cabin.

On the sixth day the storm lifted. They got busy making two sleds out of broken parts of the airplane. Captain Wilkins took sightings of the sun. Then he dropped a line through a hole in the ice to find which way they were drifting.

"Ben," he said, "five days ago when we ran out of

gas, I figured we were about seventy miles north of Point Barrow."

"We should be able to make that in a few days," Ben said cheerfully. Then he saw the look on Wilkins' face.

"The trouble is that was five days ago," the explorer said. "The wind and ocean currents have been pushing this whole floating ice pan away from Barrow, and us with it!"

Ben knew there was more. He waited for Captain Wilkins to finish. "I figure we are now about 140 miles north and east of Barrow and drifting the wrong way!" It was the kind of bad news that would make many a person quit—give up right then and there.

"We can still make it," Ben said firmly.

"You bet we can," the older explorer agreed, "and we will. Who knows? The wind and currents may even change and start us drifting toward the Alaskan shore."

They loaded the two sleds with their sleeping bags and the few supplies that were left. They started out into the biting sub-zero wind.

The trackless jumble of ice and snow stretched ahead farther than the eyes could see.

Far in the distance lay life—or death.

THE HIKE FOR LIFE
CHAPTER 19

ALL DAY long they hiked southward. Ben's frozen hand hurt so much he could not hold the sled rope. So he looped it over his shoulder and went on.

Captain Wilkins laid out the path. Once in a while he stopped to check the sun. Ben hoped the skilled explorer could set their course on the ground as well as he did in the air.

They crossed jagged ice fields. They pushed forward steadily. They had to stop now and then to fix a broken snowshoe or to melt some snow inside their mittens for drinking water.

Time after time they came to open leads of water in the ice pack. Some were narrow enough to jump over. Others they rode across on loose cakes of ice.

It was dangerous business. To fall into the water could mean death. In a matter of minutes a man would freeze stiff in his own wet clothes.

Finally Captain Wilkins called a halt to the day's hike. "I'll build a shelter for us."

He cut blocks of hard-packed snow. Carefully he laid the first blocks in a circle. He piled the others, row upon row, bending inward.

Ben helped as best he could, although his hand was nearly useless by now.

In a little over an hour they had finished the snow-house or Eskimo igloo.

"That should keep the wind off us," Captain Wilkins said. "Let's get inside."

They crawled through the small opening. Captain Wilkins pulled the last large block of snow into place after them. Soon they were warm in their sleeping bags.

The next day Captain Wilkins looked at Ben's frozen hand. He shook his head.

"Ben," he said, "I hate to tell you this, but that little finger is worthless. Poison may have set in already. It may spread. Ben, I know a little about these things. I have seen this happen before. I have my knife, Ben. If you say so—"

Ben had known for days that the little finger of his right hand could not be saved. There was still feeling in the other fingers. There was a chance for them. He smiled now. He knew it had not been easy for Captain Wilkins to bring up the idea of removing the bad finger.

"Thanks for offering, Captain," he said, "but, well—let's hold off a little while longer."

"Sure, Ben. Whatever you say."

They went on fighting their way always southward. They prayed that the wind and ocean currents would change and drive the pack ice toward the Alaskan shore.

Three days passed—four—five—a week—mile after struggling mile. Half-blinded by the glaring ice and snow, they stumbled on.

Their food supply was low. Whiskers covered their faces, turned white by the frost.

Day by day they grew weaker. They left one of the sleds behind, piling their last supplies on the other.

Each night they built a new snowhouse. Each night they crawled into their sleeping bags and wondered whether they would be alive when morning came.

They prayed together. They remembered long forgotten verses from the Bible. They found new hope in saying them. They talked of many things.

No two men had ever felt closer. No two men had ever needed each other more.

The ninth day passed. Ben lost track of time. One day was like the next. It took all their effort just to move forward slowly step by step.

Each day, each hour, it got worse and worse. Often they stumbled and lay panting in the snow. Each helped lift the other up and move on.

To lay longer in the snow would be to sleep the frozen sleep of death.

Ben was not sure what day it was that Captain Wilkins fell through a thin shell of ice into the icy sea.

Ben grabbed a rope to throw to his struggling friend so he could help drag him out of the water. Weak as he was, Wilkins had already clawed his way back onto a floating cake of ice. Then he worked his way quickly from drifting piece to drifting piece until he was again on the solid ice.

There was no time to waste. To lie down or stand still would be to freeze to death in his own wet clothes.

Quickly Wilkins took off his clothes. He started rolling them in the dry snow to blot up the water. The air bit at his naked body. Now and then he ran around in circles to keep his blood from freezing. Seeing the explorer running around naked in the snow, Ben thought Wilkins had gone mad.

Soon Wilkins was able to blot most of the water out of his clothes. He pulled them back on quickly. Then he ran around some more, swinging his arms. He was so weak it was hard to do, but he made himself keep at it.

"I've got to keep moving, Ben. I can't stop, or I'll freeze stiff."

It took quite a while. Several times Wilkins stumbled and fell to the snow. Each time he pushed himself back up and kept going.

After a time the clothes finished drying out from the heat of his body.

"Well, that's one way to keep from freezing to death," Wilkins caught his breath. Then he smiled weakly, "But I must have run ten miles doing it. In circles, at that."

"You should have headed for land, Captain," Ben said. "Ten miles in a straight line might have taken you there."

They both laughed weakly.

Wilkins said as they got ready to go on again, "When we reach land, it will be together—or not at all. Understand?"

Ben nodded. A person who met someone like George Hubert Wilkins once in a lifetime was a lucky man.

On April 16, 1927, the thirteenth day after leaving the wrecked Stinson, they sighted land. Soon they came upon dog tracks in the snow. The outline of buildings loomed in the distance.

Ben let out a wild yell. It was quickly matched by one from Captain Wilkins.

"Ben," the explorer said, "what are we going to do with this last chocolate bar?"

"Is that all the food we have left?"

"That's all. That is all we had left between us and starvation. I didn't want to tell you. You have had problems enough with that hand."

"Everything will be fine now, Captain," Ben said. "Just fine."

"I think there is something we should do right now, don't you, Ben?"

There was no need to ask what it was. Ben knew. In fact, he had been thinking of the same thing.

"Yes, sir, I do," Ben agreed.

The two men dropped to their knees in the snow and spoke their prayers of thanks to the Lord.

THE WINNING SPIRIT
CHAPTER 20

A FEW DAYS later the doctor at Barrow cut off Ben's frozen, useless finger to stop the spread of poison. The pain went away, and the rest of the hand was soon all right. Ben returned to Fairbanks. He felt lucky to have lost only a finger. It could have been his life.

While Ben was in Fairbanks, Captain Wilkins took the second Stinson airplane and tried several more flights over the polar ice. He soon found that this plane was not as good as the one he and Ben had left drifting on the arctic ice pack.

Wilkins was forced to give up the expedition. In the public's eyes, the second Detroit Arctic Expedition had failed like the first expedition.

Ben and Wilkins once more returned to the United States. "Maybe we can try again next year, Ben," the Australian explorer said, "Of course, I may run into some trouble getting more money and more airplanes. But I will try."

Ben looked proudly at this man who would not give up. "Captain, I will be waiting for your call whenever you need me."

Wilkins smiled. "I figured as much. We seem to be turning into real snow men, you and I."

"You nearly did the day you fell through the ice, Captain."

Wilkins laughed. Then he said, "Ben, don't let what the public thinks bother you," he said. "We didn't fail, at least not all the way. We learned a lot about how the arctic ice pack moves. We learned something important about how deep the Arctic Ocean is. We learned that airplanes can fly in the worst weather of the far north. We learned how to live through a long hike across the ice. To my way of thinking, that is hardly failing."

"Mine, either."

"I still think we can make that flight from Barrow to Spitsbergen. That would be something, to fly an airplane from America over the top of the world to Europe.

"It would indeed," Ben agreed. "It would prove once and for all that flying across the polar ice is the shortest and best way to reach many parts of the world."

"If I can work things out by next winter, I will get in touch with you, Ben."

"Fine," Ben said. "Good luck, sir."

The summer passed and the chill of fall came over the land. Each day Ben found himself wanting more and more to get back to Alaska.

Then one day his hopes were answered with a telephone call from Captain Wilkins. Somehow Wilkins had talked the *Detroit-News* into putting up some more money to make a third and final trip into the Arctic Blind Spot.

"This time," Captain Wilkins said over the telephone, "I want to prove just one thing—that it is possible to fly over the top of the world to Europe."

"Good, Captain," Ben replied. "I feel we can do it. After all, last year Charles Lindbergh flew nonstop all the way from New York to Paris, He did it in a single-engine plane, too."

"That's the kind we're going to have, Ben," Wilkins said. "Wait until you see it. It's called a Lockheed Vega. It's a small plane, but it's fast and strong. I sold the second Stinson and the old Fokker *Detroiter* in order to help buy the Lockheed. If any plane will carry us to Spitsbergen, I think the Lockheed will do it."

"I hope so."

"We have been through a lot together, Ben, and we're still alive. For my money, you are the best pilot for the job."

"I won't let you down."

"By the way, Ben, how is the finger?"

Ben smiled and answered, "All right, I guess. I haven't seen it since last winter when I left it at Point Barrow!"

Captain Wilkins' loud laugh filled the telephone. Ben joined in. It was a strange thing to laugh about perhaps, but he and Captain Wilkins had found a lot of things to laugh over from time to time, even when things were not the least bit funny. Ben was sure that their good cheer during some of their darkest moments had helped to keep them alive and going.

It would be good being back with his friend again. It would be good, even though to fly in the arctic was always to fly with danger at your side.

ON TO SPITSBERGEN!
CHAPTER 21

On February 26, 1928, Eielson and Wilkins were back in Fairbanks.

The Lockheed Vega was a single-engine, high-wing airplane. Its cigar-shaped body was built for speed. It was painted a bright orange color to make it easy to see against the snow or the sky.

"She is a small plane, Ben," Captain Wilkins said, "but she is faster than anything we have flown before. She has a good radio and a new kind of compass. I had more gas tanks put in, too."

"We'll need them to fly nonstop to Spitsbergen," Ben said. "Twenty-two hundred miles is a long way, and there's no place to stop in between."

"Not unless we want to take a much longer hike across the ice pack than we did last year!"

"No, thank you. Not if I can help it."

This time just the two of them were making the expedition. Money was short. Wilkins had not been able to hire mechanics, pilots, or other help.

"It is all up to us, Ben."

Three weeks later they flew the heavily loaded Lockheed Vega up to Barrow. In the narrow body of the plane Wilkins' seat and map table were set up in the cabin behind Ben.

"It gives me more room to work," Wilkins said. "I may need it to steer a course all the way to Spitsbergen."

The Eskimos and white traders at the farthest north town of Barrow were happy to see them, but some shook their heads.

"You two are going to get killed yet," they warned. "How many times do you have to fail before you will learn to give up?"

"Give up?" Captain Wilkins said, smiling. "You mean quit? Ben, what does that word mean?"

"Quit? I never heard it before, Captain," Ben said.

"I haven't either. So let's go."

The day they planned their takeoff a hard snowstorm blew down over Barrow. The storm piled snow deep on the runway. When the weather cleared, Captain

Wilkins hired a group of Eskimos to shovel a path through the snow.

In trying to take off, the Lockheed Vega skidded to one side, hit the snowbank, and broke a ski. It took several days to make a new ski. By that time the snow had come again, covering the runway. Already it seemed the third arctic expedition was going to fail.

In a few days the storm lifted, but the cold dropped to around fifty degrees below zero. The land lay frozen tight.

The natives were tired of shoveling snow, and a long clear strip was needed for the Lockheed to take off.

"They simply don't seem to care any more whether we get off or not," Captain Wilkins said. "If we can't get them to shovel a path, we're out of luck."

"I will see what I can do about it, Captain," Ben offered. "I have an idea. I used to coach a few Eskimos at Fairbanks High School. They are good basketball players, good team players. They love to win."

Ben divided the Barrow Eskimos into two teams, offering the winning team a prize.

"How do we know who wins?" one of the Eskimos asked.

"That's easy," Ben told them. "The team that shovels the longest and smoothest strip is the winner."

The natives grabbed their shovels, and the snow

began to fly. Before they finished, they had shoveled a path about fourteen feet wide and hundreds of feet long. It was not as wide as Ben would have liked, but it would do.

"I gave each team a prize," Ben told Captain Wilkins. "It looked like a tie game to me."

It was so cold that Captain Wilkins had to heat the oil over a stove before pouring it into the airplane engine.

Ben turned the switch and started the engine. He looked at the small calendar that Captain Wilkins had

pinned to the inside of the Lockheed Vega's cabin. It was April 15, 1928.

Captain Wilkins climbed into the plane and pulled the cabin door shut behind him. He took his seat at the small map table behind the pilot's seat. He leaned forward and tapped Ben on the shoulder.

"I'm ready whenever you are, Ben. We are going to head for Kings Bay or Green Harbor. Either place is all right. We will see how things go."

Ben nodded and smiled. Then he turned to the controls. It would take all the skill he had to take off

from the narrow runway the Eskimos had dug. He pushed the throttle forward. The engine roared. But the plane did not move ahead.

"The skis are stuck!" Wilkins shouted.

Ben pushed the rudder pedals from side to side. He moved the control stick all the way to the left, then to the right, forward and back. The plane rocked from side to side and up and down. Suddenly the skis broke loose from the ice. The airplane started forward.

"Hang on!" Ben shouted. But his words were lost in the roar of the engine.

The Lockheed picked up speed. It went faster and faster. One ski hit a rough spot on the ice. The plane skidded. One wing scraped against the snowbank.

Ben worked hard at the controls. The plane straightened out. They were nearing the end of the runway. Would they make it? They were carrying a very heavy load of gas.

At the last possible second Ben pulled back on the stick. The Lockheed seemed to shake itself, as though trying to break free from the snow. As the shaking stopped, the plane rose smoothly into the cold arctic sky.

Ben took a deep breath. He turned the plane slowly northward, pointing the spinning propeller toward the top of the world.

He smiled over his shoulder at Captain Wilkins who smiled back. Then the explorer's eyes turned back to the maps spread out in front of him. The course ahead would be a hard one. There was much planning for him to do in order to keep them from getting lost. There was much careful flying ahead for Ben to keep them safely in the air. Each had his job. There would be no turning back now.

It was on to Spitsbergen!

THE LONG FLIGHT
CHAPTER 22

THE POWERFUL engine of the Lockheed Vega hummed smoothly. Hour after hour the small orange airplane flew through the clear blue sky. Beneath its wings stretched miles of glaring arctic ice.

"No man has ever looked down on that before," Captain Wilkins shouted in Ben's ear. "If this weather keeps up, we should have no trouble reaching Spitsbergen."

For hours Ben hardly knew that Wilkins was in the airplane. Seated behind Ben, the explorer was busy over his maps and charts. It was necessary to change course many times as they flew over the top of the world. It took all of his time and skill to set a course that would keep them flying to Spitsbergen.

Ben thought that the new compass was acting strangely in the polar region, swinging back and forth. Turning in his seat, he told Wilkins about it.

The explorer began taking sightings on the sun to help set their course.

There was no sign of land beneath them. All that could be seen were endless miles of floating ice with a few open leads where the Arctic Ocean showed through.

Wilkins passed a note forward to Ben. "I think it is safe to say," the note read, "that there is no land under the polar pack ice. The thick ice cap floats upon the Arctic Ocean."

It was a discovery that could be very important to the world. It might even mean that someday submarines could travel under the ice pack from one side of the world to the other! Maybe, they would go right under the North Pole!

Ben grew tired of looking down upon the rough bright ice spreading out in all directions. He thought, "I would rather do my flying over land. Alaska is the place to fly. I would still like to start a real flying business there."

Ben knew that it was a wish that might very well come true if this flight turned out all right. Such a flight was sure to bring Captain Wilkins and himself some fame.

Fame itself meant nothing to Ben, but it was a strange thing what fame could do. Men listened to you

then. Often they were willing to help you make your other dreams come true. They might help Ben in his dreams of setting up a flying business in Alaska.

Now Wilkins planned a route that did not go over the North Pole, but went around it. He laid out a circling course reaching toward the distant Norwegian island of Spitsbergen.

After all, there was no point in going out of their way to the Pole. Byrd had been there. Amundsen had flown across it in his dirigible. Admiral Peary had gone there by dogsled years before the others.

"Look ahead at those clouds," Wilkins shouted. "We may be running into some bad weather."

He was right. Soon the wind was slamming against the plane. Ben fought at the controls. He climbed the Lockheed above the clouds. Now they flew on without ever seeing the ice beneath them.

They dug out their bag of food. "It's better to eat now," Wilkins called out. "We may have our hands full of bad weather pretty soon."

A few minutes later, just as he finished taking a sighting on the sun, the plane flew into some dark, churning storm clouds.

"Can we climb higher?" Wilkins shouted.

Ben tried, but the Lockheed had already climbed as high as it would go. The storm shook it around as a dog shakes a rag. Ice began to form on the wings. It made the plane very heavy. It was all Ben could do to keep the Lockheed from going into a dive. Although it was icy cold inside the cabin, sweat poured down Ben's face. His body hurt all over.

Wilkins was busy, too, studying his maps and charts and laying out the course. If they got lost now, it could mean death to both of them. There was no smooth ice or snow beneath them on which to land safely. Even if they lived through a crash landing on the jagged arctic ice, they were hundreds of miles from the nearest land.

There could be little hope of hiking out as they had done once before.

Ben lost track of time. Hour after hour he worked the controls. His arms hurt. His legs grew numb and heavy, but there was no chance to rest, not even for a minute. He could not see through the blinding snow. Chunks of ice kept breaking off the wings and slamming into the airplane.

Then suddenly there was a break in the clouds. Captain Wilkins grabbed Ben's shoulder and pointed off to the right. There were some ice-capped peaks rising sharply into the sky.

"Greenland!" Wilkins shouted. "That's Greenland! Shall we head for it and land?"

To land on Greenland might save their lives, but it would also mean they would not reach Spitsbergen. Already they were beginning to get low on gas, and Greenland was many miles off their course. "Let's keep going," Ben yelled. "On to Spitsbergen!"

Captain Wilkins smiled. Ben knew it was the answer his friend had hoped for. Yet Wilkins would not have asked him to go if Ben had not been willing.

They had flown for nearly eighteen hours, partly through bright daylight and partly through the darkness of night and the storm. Whenever he had the chance, Captain Wilkins was busy taking sightings and setting the course.

Wilkins passed a note to Ben. "We are just two hundred miles from Spitsbergen. Let's see if we can get beneath the storm."

Ben dived the Lockheed down through the clouds. He pulled out of the dive just above the storm-tossed waves of the sea. He was so close that the spray of the waves smashed into the windshield and quickly froze. Ben could not see out. He pulled the plane higher, but

the blinding ice stayed on the windshield. Then he saw that the gas gauge was getting down near the empty mark.

"No!" he cried out. "Not now! Not when we are so close!" But his cries were lost in the roar of the engine and the howling wind.

"I can't see out, Captain!" Ben shouted, trying to find a clear spot on the windshield.

"We have all the luck, don't we, Ben?" Captain Wilkins' face was grim now. It seemed that once again they were going to fail.

Ben flew on blindly, keeping his eyes on his instruments. He did not know how long he kept flying without being able to see out ahead of the plane.

Then Wilkins was pounding him on the back and pointing out a side window.

"There is land beneath us, Ben. It has to be Spitsbergen! We'd better go down."

"But it's not Kings Bay or Green Harbor. I think I can fly a while longer by instruments."

"We can't take that kind of a chance, Ben. I don't believe we are far from Green Harbor. Right now we'd better get down and clean that windshield. It shouldn't take long. Then we can go on."

Ben knew Wilkins spoke wisely. It was too risky trying to fly blind any longer.

They started down. Wilkins pressed his face against the side window and called out what to do. Somewhere ahead and below them Wilkins had spotted a fairly smooth landing spot, but Ben could not see it. He could see nothing but the instruments in front of him.

"To the left a little!" Wilkins shouted.

Ben pushed the control stick slightly to the left.

"Up, Ben! You're too low! Now to the right—careful—down a little—watch it!"

Trusting his friend completely, Ben moved the controls only when Wilkins shouted the orders.

"You're ten feet up, Ben. It looks good. Easy, boy. Get ready to cut the throttle—now—NOW!"

The skis hit the snow. The plane bounced once, came down again, and skidded to a stop.

As they climbed out of the Lockheed Vega together, Wilkins began to laugh.

"Oh, Mother Earth—we're home again! Ben, that was about as nice a landing as I've ever seen you make."

Ben smiled as he looked over the plane for any damage. There was none. He thought of all the rough landings he had made when things did get broken.

"Captain," he said, "maybe I do better when I can't see!"

GREEN HARBOR
CHAPTER 23

By the time they had scraped the ice off the windshield, the storm had become worse. The howling wind rocked the Lockheed, nearly tipping it over. They could see only a few feet through the thick snowfall.

"We can't take off in this," Captain Wilkins said. "We will just have to sit it out."

They let the oil out of the engine so that it would not freeze inside. They tied the wings down and packed snow around the skis to keep the wind from blowing the airplane away. Then they climbed back into the cabin.

Ben looked at the calendar. "This is Monday, isn't it, Captain?" he asked. "I've lost track of the time."

"That's right. It's Monday, April 16, 1928. I don't know just where we are, but I do know we're somewhere in

Spitsbergen. We made it, Ben. We made it in just twenty hours and twenty minutes, the first nonstop flight over the top of the world in an airplane."

"Finally we won, Captain."

"We surely did. And it's about time, Ben. Now let's get some rest."

For four days and nights the blizzard raged outside the airplane. It was all Ben and Captain Wilkins could do to keep from freezing to death. Much of the time they stayed inside their sleeping bags. They ate carefully of their sandwiches, chocolate bars, and the other small supply of food.

Captain Wilkins said on the fourth day, "Unless we can get out of here soon, the world may never know that we have opened up a new air route over the top of the world."

Ben had been thinking the same thing. Their food was getting low. The cold was terrible. Still they did not know just where they were. With the weather so bad, to set out on foot would mean almost sure death to them. Ben was not afraid of death, but he did not like the idea of a slow freezing death while hiking through the snow.

"When my time comes," Ben had said more than once, "I hope it comes fast and is over quickly."

On the fifth day the storm let up.

"O.K., Ben," Wilkins said, "let's see whether we can get this plane into the air again."

First they had to dig the Lockheed out of the deep snowdrifts which the blizzard had packed around it. Then they checked to see how much gas was left in the tanks.

"Twenty gallons," Ben said. "That won't take us far, sir. I hope we are near Green Harbor.[1]"

They put on their snowshoes and made a path in the deep snow for the plane's skis to follow.

They used a little of the gas to build a fire over which to heat the oil. Then Wilkins poured the hot oil in, and Ben started the engine. It ran smoothly.

Wilkins climbed in. Ben opened the throttle. The engine roared, but the plane did not move.

"The skis are stuck again!" Wilkins shouted.

Nothing that Ben did would break them loose. Ben shut the throttle. He looked back at Wilkins and shook his head.

"Look, Ben," the explorer said, "I'll get down on the ground and rock the plane back and forth. You give it full throttle. As soon as it starts to move, I'll climb back in."

"It's dangerous for you to be outside the plane like that," Ben warned.

"It's the only thing we can do, Ben. Don't worry, I'll get back in as soon as you start moving."

---
[1] Green Harbor, Spitsbergen, is now called Grønfjordbreane, Svalbard.

Wilkins made his way back toward the door in the cabin. Ben felt a blast of cold air on his back as Wilkins opened the door and jumped out onto the snow.

In a moment Ben felt the plane rocking back and forth. He knew Captain Wilkins was putting his shoulder to it, pushing, rocking, trying to break the skis free from the icy snow.

Ben opened the throttle wide. The cabin filled with the engine's loud roar. The Lockheed did not move. He pulled the throttle back, then pushed it forward again hard. Suddenly the plane moved ahead fast as the skis broke loose from their icy grip.

Ben had his hands full for the next few minutes as he tried to keep the plane's skis in the path they had made in the snow.

Faster…faster…faster.

"Up!" Ben shouted, pulling back on the control stick. "Up!"

Just as a high ridge of snow loomed ahead, the plane lifted into the air. The skis barely scraped over the top of the ridge.

"Hot dog!" Ben shouted. "We made it! On to Green Harbor!"

Carefully Ben checked the instruments. Everything seemed in order but the gas gauge. Its needle hung near the empty mark.

"If only we have enough gas," Ben thought.

He twisted around in his seat to ask Captain Wilkins to set the proper course. His eyes popped wide open. A sudden strange feeling chilled his bones.

The cabin behind him was empty!

Ben knew almost at once what had happened, Wilkins was back there, on the ground in the snow. For some reason when the plane started forward, Wilkins had not been able to climb back in as he had planned.

Ben turned the plane quickly. Would he be able to find Wilkins again? He circled over the endless white snowfield.

"I must find him. I must! I must!"

Then he saw the tiny dark dot on the snow far below. He dived down toward it.

There was Wilkins, waving up at him,

"Thank the Lord," Ben said.

He landed, Wilkins came running over to the plane. He opened the door and crawled up behind Ben.

"I'm glad you happened to be passing by, Ben," he said, grinning, "In time it would have been lonely down there."

"What happened?"

"The snow was slippery, I hadn't counted on the strong wind blast from the propeller, I couldn't climb back in after you started to move, O.K., let's try it again."

"Let's not!"

Already the skis had frozen to the snow again, Wilkins looked around and found a long piece of driftwood, "I can stand in the doorway and push with this pole, Ben," he said, "I will be more careful this time."

It was not Ben's place to go against the explorer's orders. "Just don't fall out," he warned.

Once again the Lockheed Vega began to rock back and forth as Wilkins stood in the open doorway and pushed down hard on the pole. Thus he was able to rock the plane back and forth, hoping to break the skis loose. Ben opened the throttle. But the plane would not move.

Ben quickly glanced behind him. Captain Wilkins was hanging half in and half out of the doorway of the plane. He pushed hard on the pole. The wind blast from the propeller tore at him.

Ben got ready to cut the throttle. Even though all of this was using gas, he would rather stay there and freeze than have anything happen to Wilkins.

Then with a great effort, Wilkins gave a final push. Suddenly the Lockheed moved ahead. Wilkins shouted, dropped the pole, and fell backward into the cabin. He looked up and smiled weakly at Ben.

"That's that," his lips formed the words. "On to Green Harbor!"

Once more in the air, Ben watched the gas gauge closely. Their gas would run out soon, and when it did, they might be no better off than before.

A few minutes later Wilkins pounded Ben on the shoulder and pointed through the side window.

"Radio towers!" Wilkins shouted in his ear. "Look!"

"Green Harbor!" Ben called happily. "It must be the weather station at Green Harbor!"

"We made it! We made it! Ben, you're the greatest flier in the world!"

"You're the greatest arctic explorer, Captain!"

They laughed like children.

There was not time to circle the towers. The engine began to sputter and miss. The gas gauge had reached EMPTY.

Ben picked the best spot on the snow he could see and glided down for his landing. As the plane hit, a ski broke, but the Lockheed stayed right side up as it skidded to a stop.

People began to rush out of the small group of buildings nearby. Ben and Wilkins jumped out of the plane and ran to meet them. Everyone began to talk at once.

"Where in the world are you from?" one of the men asked.

"Alaska," Captain Wilkins said simply.

"Alaska? Did you say Alaska?"

"That's right."

"But no one ever has flown an airplane from Alaska to Spitsbergen. It can't be done."

"Oh, don't be so sure," Ben said.

"We just did it," Captain Wilkins added.

"Over the arctic ice?"

"That's right. Over the top of the world."

The people looked at the tiny plane and shook their heads. Ben and Wilkins smiled at each other. Then, arm in arm, they followed the others toward the radio building. The outside world would be waiting for word from them.

Somewhere within that cluster of buildings at Green Harbor there might also be some hot soup waiting.

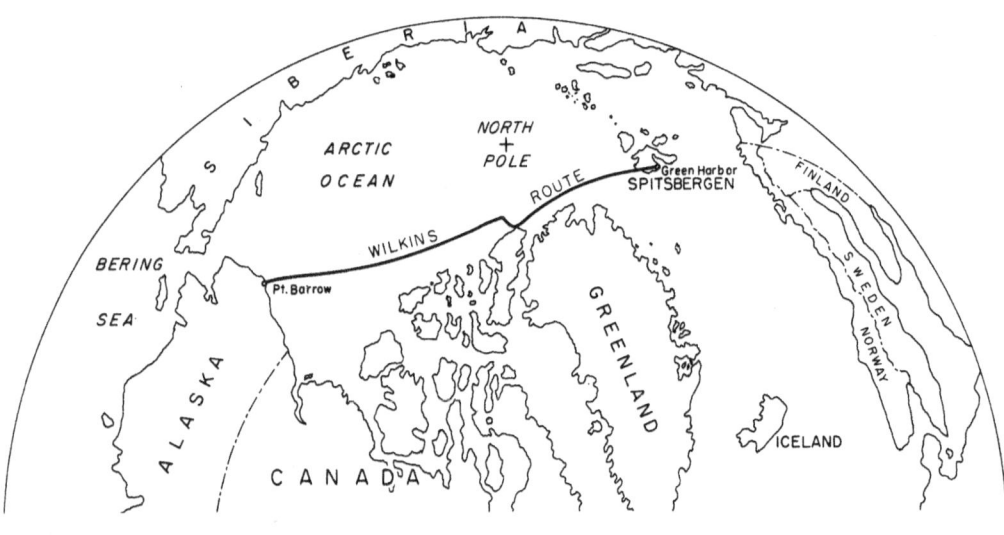

THE HEROES RETURN
CHAPTER 24

THE WINTER ICE was still thick on the water around Spitsbergen. No ships could break through it to get to Green Harbor. So Ben and Captain George Wilkins had to wait nearly three weeks. Finally the ice thawed enough to allow a Norwegian ship to get through and pick them up.

In the meantime word of their around-the-Pole flight from America to Europe had spread far and wide. Like Admiral Byrd, who had first flown to the North Pole, they were heroes. Like Charles Lindbergh, who had made the first nonstop flight across the Atlantic Ocean the year before, the world stood by to greet them.

In England, Captain George Hubert Wilkins was knighted by King George V. He was now called Sir Hubert Wilkins. The King of Norway presented Ben with the Leif Ericson Memorial Award for his part in the exploration. All over Europe the two men were given honor after honor. They were presented with many awards and medals. There were dinners and parties.

"Hurrah for Ben Eielson!"

"Hurrah for Sir Hubert Wilkins!"

Wilkins said one night when they returned tired to their hotel, "These people mean well, but enough is enough. I would like to be out on the pack ice again. I have nearly eaten myself sick. I have given so many speeches that I have run out of words."

Ben smiled. "I know what you mean. I am ready to go home or back to quiet Alaska."

"How about to the other end of the world?"

"The other end?"

"The antarctic, the South Pole."

Ben looked at his friend of many adventures. What a man Sir Hubert Wilkins was! After all the hardships they had shared during the past three years, the explorer was ready and eager for more.

"I'm not fooling, Ben," Wilkins said. "Think it over. No airplane has ever been to the antarctic before. There is much mapping and charting to do for that area and many important discoveries to be made."

"Well," Ben said, "I still hope to go back to Alaska and start a real flying business there. I want to get

several planes, the more the better. I want to fly all over the territory, not to just a few towns and villages. I want to fly even to the most distant spots. Alaska needs airplanes more than ever."

"You'll do it, Ben," Sir Hubert said. Then he smiled. "Now that you're a world hero, I'll bet you won't have any trouble raising the money to help you."

"I hope you are right, Captain."

"Anyway, Ben, think about that South Pole trip. We wouldn't be gone long. You can always go back to Alaska."

"I will think about it," Ben agreed.

On board a ship headed across the Atlantic Ocean toward the United States they enjoyed a few days of much-needed rest. But as soon as they landed in New York, the merry-go-round started again. There were more parties and speeches, more honors and awards.

The best thing about it all was that Ben's father and younger brother came east to meet him. They hugged each other eagerly. Ben was warmed by the proud smiles on their faces.

Later Ben and Sir Hubert Wilkins took off in the Lockheed Vega, which had been fixed, and flew west toward Hatton, stopping at cities along the way. They were welcomed as heroes.

"Ben," Sir Hubert said one day, "I guess this is all part of waking up and finding you are a hero in the eyes of the world."

"I don't feel any different," Ben said. "Maybe I'm a little more tired. But that's all."

His friend laughed. "I am, too. The people pick the heroes though, Ben. You and I had very little to say about it."

On the morning after Ben became thirty-one years old, he landed the Lockheed Vega on the same hayfield where he had landed the Jenny nine years earlier. He could not help thinking of how many things had happened during those years.

The people of Hatton would long remember the celebration they put on for "Our own hero, Ben!" and for Sir Hubert Wilkins.

Everyone Ben knew was there. Among them were the members of the old Hatton Aero Club.

"Our hero, Ben!" they shouted.

He and Garvin Olson pounded each other happily on the back. They remembered just a few years ago a hero was anyone who dared climb into an airplane.

That night Ben was back with his family.

A few days later Sir Hubert Wilkins returned east to get ready for his trip to the antarctic.

Ben stayed in Hatton for the next few weeks, but each day he grew a little more restless. He had talked to several men in New York about helping him start a new aviation company in Alaska. They had listened. They had even nodded their heads as though they thought the idea a good one. They had asked Ben to give them a little time to make up their minds. But no word came.

Once again Ben said good-by to his family and caught the train east. When he arrived in New York, he was surprised to find his friend Joe Crosson there. The tall, good-looking bush pilot smiled. "I thought you knew, Ben," he said. "Sir Hubert Wilkins sent me a telegram in Alaska. He wondered whether I wanted to fly one of the planes on the antarctic expedition. I jumped at the chance, and here I am."

"One of the planes?"

"Where have you been, Ben? Didn't you know that Wilkins has two Lockheed Vegas for the flights over the antarctic? The Hearst newspapers are paying for the expedition."

"I'm afraid I haven't been keeping up very well on Sir Hubert's plans, Joe."

"Haven't been keeping up? But you are going, aren't you? Wilkins said you are to be his number one pilot."

Ben smiled. "I hadn't even made up my mind to go," he said. "You see, Joe, there is some other business I have in mind."

"Sure, I know, Ben. I want to go back to Alaska, too, but that can wait a few months. How often does a fellow get the chance to fly around the South Pole? You'd better think it over."

Ben thought it over, and the more he thought, the more excited he became over the idea of going to the antarctic.

"We can both go to Alaska when we get back," Joe Crosson said. "We might even go into business together, Ben."

Ben smiled. Joe was quite a fellow, a real friend!

"Do you know where I can reach Sir Hubert?" Ben asked.

"I thought you might want to know," Crosson said, grinning. "I just happen to have his telephone number right here."

"Very handy," Ben laughed. "I guess you knew I couldn't turn down a chance to go to the antarctic."

Ben picked up the telephone and called Sir Hubert's hotel.

"Oh, I wasn't worried about your not going, Ben," the explorer's cheerful voice came over the telephone. "You have adventure in your blood, just as I have. You could no more keep away from the antarctic then I could! You just needed a little time to think it over."

"Maybe you're right," Ben said. Sir Hubert's laugh came over the telephone.

On September 22, 1928, the Wilkins-Hearst Antarctic Expedition boarded a ship carrying men, planes, and supplies. Pulling up anchor, the ship left the New York harbor and sailed south toward the bottom of the world!

BOTTOM OF THE WORLD
CHAPTER 25

It took six weeks of sailing to reach the pack ice of the antarctic.

"It looks about the same as the pack ice up in the arctic, doesn't it?" Joe Crosson said. They stood on the ship's deck and looked across the great floating ice fields.

"It really does, Joe," Ben agreed. "Ice is ice, no matter which end of the earth it's on."

Sir Hubert Wilkins was standing nearby. "There is quite a difference between the northern arctic, fellows, and the southern antarctic. As Ben and I learned, there is no land under the ice and snow around the North Pole—just ocean."

"At least we are quite sure," Ben said.

"We know there is land around the South Pole," Wilkins added. "I have been here before. you know. I have climbed some of the mountains. They are mighty big and rugged. There are many glaciers between the mountains. There is plenty of land down here."

"I don't imagine it's very good for farming, though," Joe Crosson said.

"Hardly," Wilkins laughed.

Soon the ship was smashing its way through the ice pack, backing up and slamming forward, backing up again and slamming forward again. Little by little the ship moved ahead.

Finally, on November 8, the ship arrived in the antarctic. Men, planes, and supplies were unloaded. A base camp was set up.

For the next two weeks bad weather kept the expedition pinned down. Ben and Joe hiked around the snow-covered land. They watched great numbers of antarctic birds.

They played with the funny-looking, friendly penguins. These strange nonflying birds gave them many laughs.

"They look as if they're about to go out to a fancy dinner, don't they, Ben?" Joe Crosson said.

"Yes, black coat, white vest, and all."

On November 22 the weather got better.

"Let's get one of the Lockheed Vegas ready to go, Ben," Wilkins said. "We'll make just a short hop today."

A few hours later they took off. Sitting behind Ben, Sir Hubert looked happily out the window.

"This is really something, isn't it, Ben?" he shouted above the roar of the engine. "Here we are flying over the bottom of the world in the very same plane we flew over the top of the world!"

"Oh, we get around, don't we?" Ben called back.

Soon they returned to the base camp and made a smooth landing on the icy runway.

"Now you've done it, Ben," Wilkins said, shaking his hand. "You have piloted the first airplane ever to fly over the antarctic!"

There was great joy at the base camp that night. Huddling around the stoves, the men listened in on the long-range radio as news of the flight was being spread around the world. Ben's name was spoken along with Wilkins'.

"Good for you, Ben," Joe Crosson said. "You have earned all the good things they are saying about you, my bush-flying friend."

It was a great honor Ben knew.

During the coming days Ben's job was to fly Sir Hubert Wilkins on ever longer hops across the antarctic.

Joe Crosson also flew the second Lockheed Vega. Flying in first one plane and then the other, Wilkins kept busy making maps and charts. He also studied the strange antarctic weather.

Each day he reported his findings by radio to the rest of the world. Ever deeper they flew inland. They went closer and closer to the South Pole.

The vast ice fields beneath their wings were cut up by great dark cracks. Often Ben flew down low to the ice. He could see that the cracks seemed to have no bottom.

"I hope we never have to make a landing down there," Ben called to Wilkins.

"So do I, Ben. This is a lot more rugged country than the arctic."

Day after day, flight after flight, new discoveries were made.

Christmas came. The men of the expedition set up their Christmas tree. It was made of metal strips and tin cans and whatever other bright and colorful things they could make or find. It was the best they could do, for not a single green thing grew from the rocky land of the frozen antarctic.

The men of the expedition traded presents and sang Christmas songs. Over the radio they spoke to their families back home in the United States.

A week later the year 1928 ended. The good flying weather also came to an end.

"It's time to pack up and head for home," Sir Hubert Wilkins said. "We will leave the airplanes here as well as the few supplies that are left over. Someday I hope to come back and explore deeper toward the South Pole."

Late in January the men boarded the ship and headed north—and home.

THE *NANUK*
CHAPTER 26

BY THE MIDDLE of March, 1929, the Wilkins-Hearst Antarctic Expedition was back in New York. Another round of dinners, speeches, honors, and awards began.

"This is a part of the price you pay for success, Ben," Sir Hubert Wilkins said cheerfully. "I guess it's worth it. We have made some important discoveries during the past few years. We have found out things that men have wanted to know for a long time, things that will be of great help to men in coming years."

Ben knew that his friend was right. He was proud to have had a part in the discoveries.

At the first chance he went home to North Dakota. Again Hatton welcomed its well known flier. After a few weeks with his family, Ben became restless again.

"What's the matter with you, Ben?" Elma asked. "Every time you come back to Hatton it is the same story. You are here for a little while. We have a lot of fun together. Then you start pacing back and forth like an animal in a cage. What's the matter?"

"I'm sorry, Elma," Ben said. "There is really nothing the matter. But I—I keep thinking of Alaska. There is so much left to be done there, so much that airplanes could do."

"You want to go back there again, don't you, Ben?"

Ben smiled. "Yes, Elma, I do. Alaska is a wonderful place."

"I thought it was pretty wild, Ben."

"Right now it is, but someday it will be tamed. I think aviation will be the thing that will tame it."

"Airplanes! Airplanes!" Elma said. "You never will get over flying, will you, Ben?"

"I am afraid not, Elma, not as long as I live."

"Don't talk that way, Ben," his sister replied. "You are still a young man. You have many years ahead of you."

"I hope so, Elma," Ben said. "But even if I am not that lucky, it would not really bother me. I have seen the world from end to end. I have done what I wanted to do."

Ole Eielson had not said anything for some time. Now he smiled proudly. "Son," he said, "I have always been against your flying. I have always been afraid you would get killed. Maybe I am still afraid of it. But, Ben, I will no longer try to stop you."

"Thanks, Dad. You have always been a great father."

"So, Ben," his father said, "if you go back to Alaska, you go with our blessings." Ole Eielson turned his head to hide the tears.

When he left Hatton, Ben went back to Washington, D.C., where one of the biggest thrills of his life awaited him. He was presented the Harmon Trophy by President Herbert Hoover. The Harmon Trophy was given to him for the top-of-the-world flight to Spitsbergen in 1928.

Charles Lindbergh had received the Harmon Trophy the year before for his nonstop flight across the Atlantic Ocean.

From Washington, Ben went to New York, where he talked with important men about starting an aviation business in Alaska. This time they made up their minds quickly. They signed the papers that Ben needed to start the new business.

Early in the summer of 1929 Ben was back in Fairbanks, Alaska. Mechanic Earl Borland hurried to greet him. So did many other friends, among them Joe Crosson. He had returned to Alaska shortly after the Wilkins-Hearst Antarctic Expedition.

Ben set about buying several of the small aviation companies which had sprung up around Fairbanks. From them he formed a larger company, called Alaskan

Airways. Earl Borland came to work for him. Joe Crosson helped Ben in every way he could.

"You'll be so tied down by business, Ben," he said, "that you will have little time to fly."

Ben smiled. "You're right, Joe. In fact, I told my bosses back east that I would stay on the ground most of the time and run the new company."

"You may not find it easy to stay on the ground, Ben. You love to fly too much. It's been a long time since you got lost in an airplane."

Ben laughed. "How could I?" he said. "Sir Hubert Wilkins always set a good course for me. I wish he was up here now."

"Well, if I know him, Wilkins is probably out discovering new parts of the world."

From the start Alaskan Airways did a fair amount of business. New routes were set up. New parts of Alaska were being reached by the planes.

Then, one cold day in October word came that the American fur-trading ship *Nanuk* was caught in the ice off East Cape, on the coast of Russian Siberia. There were fifteen people trapped aboard along with a million dollars worth of arctic furs.

The owners of the ship offered Alaskan Air ways fifty thousand dollars to fly across the frozen Bering Sea and bring the people and furs safely to Alaska.

"This is our company's big chance to do something special," Ben said.

"It's a bad time of year to try flying across the Bering Sea, Ben," Joe Crosson reminded him. "There are lots of storms out there. No one has ever tried flying across the Bering Sea in winter."

"Well, I am going to try to make it in our new Hamilton airplane."

"You? Ben, I thought you were staying on the ground."

"Not this time," Ben said. "It may be dangerous, Joe. I couldn't ask a man to do a job that I couldn't do myself."

Nothing could change Ben's mind.

He called Earl Borland. "We could run into trouble."

"There is always that chance," Borland said. "I don't mind running into it as much as I would mind running away from it. I'll go."

They made the all-metal Hamilton airplane ready for the trip. They flew west to Teller, a small town on the Alaskan coast. There was gas at Teller and a place to eat and sleep.

"From here," Ben said as they tied the plane down on the windy Teller runway, "it is about three hundred miles across the Bering Sea to East Cape and the *Nanuk*."

A day later an Alaskan Airways Stinson arrived at Teller to help.

"We will have to work fast," Ben said. "The weather reports show a big storm coming this way. There is no time to waste."

The next morning the storm had begun to gather when the two planes took off for North Cape. By careful flying they were able to keep out of the storm's path. Within a few hours they reached the icebound *Nanuk*.

Ben took six passengers in the Hamilton. The pilot of the Stinson loaded his plane with a cargo of furs. The two planes started back to Alaska together.

Before they had left the Siberian coastline, a blizzard caught them. Howling winds tossed the planes around in the sky. The snow beat against their windshields, and ice began to form on the wings.

"We had better land and wait this thing out," Ben shouted to Earl.

"Land where?" the young mechanic called back. "I can't even see the ground!"

Carefully, Ben flew low. Then there came a break in the clouds. Ben circled through it, searching for a place to land.

"There, Ben!" Earl pointed out the window.

Below was a small native village. It stood out dark against the endless white of the frozen land. Nearby was a fairly smooth stretch of snow.

Ben brought the plane in for a landing. In a few minutes the Stinson followed him down.

The storm lasted for several days. Then the weather cleared. They took off again, reaching Alaska without more trouble.

Again the weather turned bad. At times the cold dropped to sixty degrees below zero. Wind, fog, snow, and ice made flying too dangerous.

Yet there was still a big job to do. There were more people and more furs to bring back. Although the people on the icebound *Nanuk* had cheerfully agreed to wait for the next trip of the Hamilton, Ben was worried about them. While the blizzard raged outside, he was as always restless and paced back and forth in his room.

FOLDED WINGS
CHAPTER 27

During the next week several more Alaskan Airways planes made their way to Teller to help with the job, but that was as far as they got. The weather westward across the Bering Sea was the worst that the natives of Teller had seen for years.

"If it ever lets up," one of the pilots said, "I guess Ben figures we can all fly over to the *Nanuk* and bring the rest of the people and furs back in one or two trips. I would say our boss is really using his head."

The days dragged on, dark, gloomy, storm-filled days. The men crowded around the trading post stove, waiting. Whenever the weather allowed, they took off. Time after time they went only a few miles over the frozen Bering Sea when a storm would drive them back to Teller.

The winter nights became longer with only a few hours of dim daylight to break the arctic darkness.

The men grew restless. They talked a lot among themselves.

"If this weather doesn't break soon, Ben had better give up," one of them said.

Whatever Ben's weaknesses might be, giving up was not one of them. He paced the floor a lot, stopping now and then to stare out the window into the raging storm.

Every day Earl Borland worked on the Hamilton.

"Whenever Ben is ready, the plane will be ready," he said proudly, "and so will I."

On November 9, 1929, the storm broke up over Teller, but the cold stayed far below zero.

"We can take off from here all right," one of the pilots said. "But look out there to the west. Over the Bering Sea it looks just as stormy and bad as ever."

"Even so," another said, "we'd better put on our warmest clothes. The boss will want us to take off for the *Nanuk*."

It was not Ben Eielson's way to ask others to do the dangerous work. He looked at the sky. A slight smile showed on his mouth. Then he looked off across the Bering Sea and shook his head. "I really can't tell what it is like out there until I go and see for myself."

Each day Ben had worried a little more about the nine people still left on the icebound fur ship. Although they had been comfortable enough when he had left them, they had hoped he would come right back. But the long raging storm had kept him from doing it. There was no telling what had happened. The ice might have crushed the ship. The people might have run out of food. They might be freezing. The storm had made it hard to use the radio.

Ben put on his warmest clothes and went to look for Earl. He found him outside working on the Hamilton. What a great, hard-working fellow Earl Borland was, he thought.

The mechanic looked up at him. Then he glanced at the sky and smiled.

"You don't need to tell me, Ben," he said. "I can see it on your face. You want to try making it to the *Nanuk*. Right?"

Ben laughed to think that Earl could read his thoughts like that. "If the plane is ready," he said.

"Oh, the plane is ready. So am I."

"I thought maybe I would go alone this time," Ben said. "That way I will have more room and can bring back a bigger load."

"Now, Ben," Earl said, "you don't mean that. If you ever needed a mechanic along with you, this is the time."

"Oh, I'm not such a bad mechanic myself."

"You're not such a good mechanic, either," the other man said. "If you have engine trouble on that ice pack, you are going to need a good mechanic. I want to go with you, Ben."

"It may get rough. Earl."

"We have flown together before when it was rough. How many flights up here in the arctic aren't rough?"

"O.K., Earl, you win."

"I'll have everything ready in a few minutes," Borland said.

"I will help," Ben offered. "We will load in more cans of gas. We will take along plenty of food and clothing, just in case…"

Less than an hour later Ben and his mechanic climbed into the cabin of the Hamilton. Darkness was closing in again. The icy wind whipped across the runway.

"Ben had better change his mind," one of the pilots said who was watching from the edge of the runway. "That storm is far from over."

"This is easy weather to get lost in," another said. "I have known Ben to get lost when there was no wind and the sun was shining."

As he warmed the engine, Ben Eielson did not hear any of this, nor did he think of it. He had learned a lot about flying a straight course from Sir Hubert Wilkins. He had a good set of instruments in the Hamilton, although even new instruments sometimes went wrong.

Still, Ben had no doubt that they would reach the *Nanuk*. He looked at his friend sitting beside him in the cabin of the plane.

"All set, Earl?"

"All set!"

Ben waved out the window at the men standing in the snow. They would follow as soon as he had reached the Nanuk and had sent back word that everything was all right.

Ben pushed the throttle forward. The powerful engine roared. The propeller tore at the wind. The plane sped ahead, faster and faster. Ben pulled back on the stick. The heavily loaded Hamilton bounced once, then lifted into the darkening sky.

The men on the ground at Teller watched as the airplane climbed higher and higher. They watched as it turned gently toward the west, toward the Bering Sea, toward the *Nanuk*.

They watched, and they thought of all that Ben Eielson had done for aviation in Alaska. They thought of the many dangers he had faced and of the many times his skill and bravery had pulled him through.

They thought of Ben as Alaska's pioneer bush pilot, Alaska's greatest flier.

They were proud of him.

The icy wind stung their faces. They watched the Hamilton, with Ben Eielson and Earl Borland in the cabin, climb toward the storm clouds which began to fill the sky.

They saw the wings of the plane tip sharply for a moment. It might have been caused by a blast of wind. It might have been Ben showing his joy in flying. It was the life he had chosen, the life he loved.

Then the airplane straightened out and flew off with Ben's firm hand on the stick.

They watched as the plane flew into the clouds… forever!

The airplane carrying Carl Ben Eielson and mechanic Earl Borland never reached the ship *Nanuk*.

Days became weeks, and weeks turned into months. Still there was no word. Yet knowing how often Ben had returned from dangers, hope still lived.

The Hamilton had carried plenty of gas and supplies. With care, men could live for a long time on the arctic ice pack. Storms came and went. Whenever possible, aircraft flew out from Teller to search for Ben and Earl. Other planes flew to the *Nanuk* and carried the people to safety. Pilots from all over Alaska, from the United States, and even from Russia rushed forward to aid in the search for the two lost fliers. Among these searching pilots was Ben's long-time friend, Joe Crosson.

Two and a half months passed. Still the search went on.

"Somehow Ben has always made it back before," the men said. "He never gave up hope. We must not."

Then, on January 25, 1930, Joe Crosson was searching the pack ice off the coast of Siberia. Far below he saw the flash of metal. He dived down and saw part of the wrecked Hamilton airplane sticking up through the snow. Its wings were folded back, as if torn by a terrible crash.

Unseen beneath the snow lay the bodies of two brave men. The search had ended.

Carl Ben Eielson, the father of aviation in the far north, the pioneer of Alaskan air trails, had made his last flight.